INTERPRETING
LITERATURE

INTERPRETING LITERATURE

History · Drama and Fiction
Philosophy · Rhetoric

KNOX C. HILL

The University of Chicago Press
Chicago & London

Library of Congress Catalog Card Number: 66-13873
THE UNIVERSITY OF CHICAGO PRESS, CHICAGO & LONDON
The University of Toronto Press, Toronto 5, Canada
© *1966 by The University of Chicago*

Preface

This book aims to help the general reader improve his ability to interpret different works of literature. How it attempts this can be suggested by comparing the range of literature to the spectrum. We could speak of history, drama, fiction, philosophy, and even of rhetoric as segments of this spectrum; and we could think of particular literary works as points within the segments. I do not say that the spectrum of literature is exhausted by the segments treated in this book. And of course I do not claim that the particular works discussed even begin to exhaust the segments they are meant to exemplify. In fact, I do not hold that any particular work really "belongs" on one point of the spectrum.

I do hold that a single work can display several structural features. For example, a work we might call a history can have dramatic, narrative, philosophical, and rhetorical features; these features can partially determine the structure of that work. Similarly, plays and novels can be historical or philosophical; novels can be dramatic, and plays can be narrative. Nevertheless, the ability to read can be improved if these different structural features are distinguished, and if the reader will develop—one at a time—distinct disciplines corresponding to those features. The structure of most great books is chiefly determined by one such feature or another. I have chosen particular works (e.g., *Macbeth*) to be subjects of analytical interpretations that bring out dramatic, philosophical, or rhetorical principles of literary structure.

Each selected work represents at best only one point on the spectrum of literature. Therefore the reader cannot expect to learn to understand drama by understanding a single play, *Macbeth,* or the works of a single playwright, like Shakespeare. But a reader who learns to carry an analysis through *Macbeth,* and at the same time develops his ability to read and think for himself, can put his understanding to use in applying the same kind of analysis to another play. Or, if the other play does not lend itself to the same kind of analysis, he can learn to recognize that fact, and seek a more appropriate approach.

The book assumes that its readers can already read better than first- or second-year college students, but less well than graduate students ought to read. Unlike Edward W. Rosenheim's *What Happens in Literature,* Grosvenor Cooper's *Learning To Listen,* and Joshua C. Taylor's *Learning To Look* (all three published by the University of Chicago Press), which were designed for students entering college, this book is designed for readers beyond that level. It stops short, however, of a higher level involving criticism and judgment. That is why the term *interpreting* is in the title, and is used extensively in the text. There is no "pure" interpretation that can be obtained without recourse to judgment. Still, it can be useful to center one's attention upon the problem of interpreting, as this book asks its readers to do.

There are, of course, some things that are said in this book and also in *What Happens in Literature.* The two books are nevertheless very different. Consistently with his purpose, Professor Rosenheim calls attention to many considerations that should enter the reader's mind as he expands his experience of imaginative literature. I select a few of these and follow them out at some length, trying to arrive at a comparatively complete interpretation in each case. I go beyond the limits of imaginative literature, but, if I am right in thinking that a single work may have its structure partially determined by several different principles, practice in historical, philosophical, and rhetorical analysis can help the reader toward a fuller understanding also of imaginative literature.

I owe thanks to more people than I can possibly name because many of the ideas in the book grew out of some twenty years of experience with the "Humanities 2" course at the University of Chicago. I owe much to many of my colleagues in that course. I wish there were some adequate way to express what I owe to the wonderfully stimulating students at the University of Chicago, in the general humanities courses, and in the philosophy courses I have been privileged to teach.

I must mention a particular debt to Professor Russell B. Thomas, who has probably done more work than anyone else on writings that were in a sense earlier versions of this one. I have borrowed heavily from him in the essay on history. I want also to thank two former students who encouraged me to complete the writing of the book and helped by giving their reactions to earlier drafts, Simon Aronson and David Snodgrass.

Contents

Chapter 1

Introduction

There are many ways to understand what is written or said. We understand a signpost properly when we take it to be pointing to something. We may think we understand other things properly when we feel that they have taught us moral lessons, as the Duke in Shakespeare's *As You Like It* "Finds tongues in trees, books in the running brooks, /Sermons in stones, and good in everything." And so in literature, we may properly take pieces of descriptive writing to be pointing, as it were, to the objects which they describe; other writings, like sermons, may be properly understood when the reader learns moral lessons from them. But there are some books which cannot be adequately understood in either way. There is something unsatisfactory about taking a play or a novel to be pointing to something; and although it may seem proper to seek profound lessons in a play or novel, attempts to formulate lessons nearly always result in the enunciation of platitudes, no matter how good the novel or play.

The essential meaning of a book may be as elusive as the personality of a man or woman. We build up our understanding of people by noticing what they say and do; but we may tragically misunderstand our dearest friend if we fail to grasp the intentions which lie back of his words or deeds. A book, too, may be misunderstood, unless its words are taken as they were intended to be taken. Certain remarks of polite conversation illustrate the fact that the grasp of literal meaning does not guarantee a proper understanding of words. No urbane person takes literally the common question, "How do you do?" To misunderstand this question is not simply to misconstrue the meaning of the words. These words can

I

literally mean: "What is the state of your health?" The person who "understands" the question in this way really misunderstands, for he attributes a literal meaning to words which the speaker does not intend to be taken literally.[1]

It may seem that in order to avoid misunderstanding an author we have only to ask him what he meant. But even a good author who knows well what he is trying to do may not be able to give a simple explanation of his intentions. Great artists are usually reluctant even to attempt explanations of their words. If they are pressed for explanations they may either stubbornly refuse to give them or may make no more than partial statements of their purposes. The complete statement of what is intended by a book can be found only in the complete book, if it is a good book.

We can gain an understanding of a subject if we understand a book that gives an accurate account of that subject; but we can develop our ability to understand the meaning of a book even if the book is inaccurate with respect to its subject. This is only to say that we should know what should be stressed in developing the discipline of reading. We cannot ignore the subject matter of the books we read. We must read in order to learn about subjects, even before we have mastered the art of reading. But it is good discipline in reading to make sure, first of all, that we understand what a book means to say. The same principle applies to the evaluation of books. As we gain understanding of a book it is hard to avoid forming an opinion about its value; but it is prudent to postpone passing judgment and to concentrate first on interpreting the book, on understanding its meaning.

Sound evaluations can be made only on the basis of understanding. In moving from understanding to criticism the reader will not, of course, leave his understanding where it was; his more critical attitude will raise it to a higher level. Furthermore, his new level of understanding may differ not only in degree but in kind. For, in becoming more critical he ought to become more sensitive to different ways of approaching literature.

[1] Drama and fiction can sharpen our sensitivities, because they contain so much dialogue which carries far more than merely literal meaning.

The method of interpretation emphasized in this book bears directly upon problems most likely to face the general reader; it also bears upon problems which are the special concern of the more scholarly reader. Many books cannot be adequately understood without research of one kind or another. The reader may need special knowledge about the lives and times of authors, or of the traditions within which they wrote. Research is often necessary to resolve difficulties readers encounter in trying to understand the structure of a book. The scholar who knows something about Elizabethan England, something which Shakespeare's *King Lear* does not tell him, may use this knowledge to illuminate such things as the use of the character of the Fool, or the attitude of Kent toward Oswald and Cornwall. He may apply his special knowledge to questions such as, How does the Fool function in relation to other elements in the play? It is questions like this that we stress. The answers may come from a perceptive reading of the book itself or sometimes may require special knowledge gained outside the book.

The general character of the mode of reading we will consider may be inferred from the above. We shall be mainly concerned with what can be found in the books themselves. We shall try to find our problems there, and to resolve them so far as possible by referring to what can be found there. We must, however, be cautious about distinguishing what is internal from what is external to a book. Consider, for example, the problem of the meaning of terms. If a reader is totally ignorant of the meaning of a word, that word can add nothing to what he finds in the book; he must go outside the book (say, to a dictionary) before the word can become, for him, a part of the book. But merely consulting a dictionary will not in itself make the word a part of the book he is reading. He will still have to make the best possible sense out of the word in the context in which he first found it. Even a reader who already knows the meaning of a word has learned this meaning through his experience of the word, and this experience is in a sense "outside" the book. Furthermore, his experience is not exactly the same as any other person's experience, and no word will mean precisely the same thing for any two people. So, although it is possible to make a working distinction between what is "internal" and what is "external" to a book, the distinction is not a simple one. The complexity of this matter can be illustrated by considering the word *conscience* in the line from *Hamlet*: "Thus conscience does make cowards of us all." The ordinary reader may find no problem here, especially if he knows only one meaning for the word and has no difficulty making sense out of it in the context. The scholar, on the other hand, knows several meanings for it, and is in a better position to interpret it most meaningfully. He may choose the meaning "knowledge" (i.e., con-science), not merely because he knows that Shakespeare and his contemporaries used it in this sense, but also because he believes this meaning fits the context better than any other. The point here is not to decide what is the best interpretation of the word, but rather to show that there can be arguments about the meaning of a word and that it is hard to say how much these arguments depend upon what is "internal" or "external" to a book.

These cautions should not lead us to restrict unduly the scope of our analyses. We may quite reasonably infer facts and meanings which are not expressly presented in the book. For example, many novels and plays do not contain remarks about what is going on "inside" the characters of the book, but we can still discover the thoughts and feelings of a given character by making reasonable inferences from what he says or does. From what is found inside *King Lear* it is reasonable to infer that Kent detests the Duke of Cornwall, although neither he nor anyone else says so.

The reader who wishes to improve his understanding of books will profit from analyzing many different kinds of literature. This book is not concerned with a precise differentiation of literature into kinds, but there are conventional ways of classifying which it will be convenient to use. Authors write for different reasons, and some of their many reasons can be grouped together. Historians claim to be giving accounts of men who actually lived and of events which actually happened at more or less precisely determined times and places. Scientists claim to be stating something about the nature of things, without the same sort of reference to time and place. Novelists and dramatists are not easy to characterize in these terms. They are not as indifferent as scientists to time and place, but what they have to say is significantly different from the historian's assertion that General Robert E. Lee surrendered with his army to General Ulysses S. Grant at Appomattox Court House on April 9, 1865.

The way in which we understand an author's purpose, therefore, will affect the way in which we interpret his book, for if we misunderstand his purpose we cannot know what he meant to say. Since there are many kinds of writing and since the ability to read one kind does not necessarily guarantee an ability to read other kinds, so the reading of various kinds of writing requires practice in reading each of them. The right approach to a given book is like the right key to a given lock. If, through experience in reading books of many different kinds, we develop a fairly complete set of approaches to literature, we stand a good chance of being able to understand any given book.

Sometimes the reading of a given book may be enriched if the reader attempts to interpret it in more than one way. For example, Plato's *Apology* and *Phaedo* are usually thought to be intended as philosophical arguments, but the student may increase his understanding of these works if he looks for dramatic elements in them, and if he is careful to relate the drama to the philosophy.

The ability to read, then, may be developed by practice in reading very different books. I do not suggest any particular order in which different books should be read. (I do think, however, that the reading skills stressed in the last two chapters, on philosophy and rhetoric, are more difficult than those described in the first two. I think the chapter on rhetoric carries the reader to a comparatively high level of reflective reading, and furthermore it can be readily applied to all literature.) Nor is there anything final in a division of books into histories, dramas, and novels; there is something unique about every great book, and analysis may help us experience this uniqueness.

The modes of analysis described in the chapters to follow are peculiarly appropriate to certain kinds of books. Besides these special modes of analysis there are many questions which can be asked of any book. These questions may be grouped under four headings.

1. All intelligent reading raises questions about the meaning of terms, kinds of sentence structure, differences of mood, distinctions between literal and figurative expressions, differences in style. The reader should have developed the habit of asking these questions before he reaches the level of reading assumed in this book, but he cannot read analytically without constantly exercising this habit; and constant exercise of a habit will tend to perfect it.

2. Analysis raises questions about the structure of a book, about the relation of its parts to one another and to the whole. For to analyze is to break down into parts. Any complex piece of writing can be well understood only if it is analyzed. A book can be analyzed in many ways, and not all analyses are equally good. An inadequate analysis could produce a mere collection of fragments. A reader could in some measure understand each of these fragments without really understanding either the parts or the whole. The elements of a collection are not really parts, since the term *part* is a relative term which has no meaning at all when separated from its correlative term, *whole* (just as the terms *father, husband, employer*, are meaningless apart from their correlatives, *child, wife, employee*). A good analysis, then, will make parts intelligible as parts, and will bring about an understanding of the whole as a whole.

The idea of analysis should not be restricted to breaking a book up into such parts as chapters, paragraphs, or sentences; or acts, scenes, or lines. There are other parts which cut across these divisions. The characters of a play or novel may appear in several chapters or scenes; yet they can be distinguished from one another, and from other kinds of parts such as plot and style. Several threads of a single narrative, running through several chapters, may be distinguished in a novel or history; different lines of argument may be distinguished in a piece of rhetoric or philosophy, and the divisions between these lines need not be like the divisions between chapters. Even if the two kinds of division seem to go together in some cases—for example, if one line of argument is confined to one

6

chapter and is presented with its own distinctive style—it may still be possible to separate the argument and the style analytically.

The student should assume that there may be one or more good reasons why any given detail is in a book and is placed where it is. He should ask what principle determines the ordering of the parts in relation to one another and the whole book. If he finds that several principles seem to account for a given detail, he should ask whether they are all of equal importance, or whether some are subordinate to others or even if one principle is of pre-eminent importance. Consider this with reference to a brief passage from *Macbeth*:

> Before my body
> I throw my warlike shield. Lay on, Macduff,
> And damn'd be him that first cries, Hold, enough!

If we ask why the word *enough* was chosen we may answer that it rhymes with Macduff, it is accented like Macduff, it fits into a line of iambic pentameter, it has a literal meaning which suits the author's purpose, and it has an emotional quality which is appropriate for the situation. Now there are many words which have one or another of these many characteristics. Perhaps no word except *enough* has so many characteristics which fit it for this particular place. So it may appear that neither rhyme, accent, rhythm, literal meaning, nor emotional quality is pre-eminent but that *enough* is chosen simply because it suits them all. But why should they all function here? Why, for example, should there be rhyme? The passage is neither preceded nor followed by rhyming lines, and the sudden appearance of rhyme seems itself to have to be accounted for on some other principle. Perhaps, also, there is some definite reason why iambic pentameter is used. These particular questions about rhyme and meter are not difficult, but this line of questioning can be pushed very far, even about a single word; and it can be fruitfully applied to much larger parts.

Along with these questions the reader may ask how complete a book is. Are there gaps in the book's structure? Is it impossible to find any connection between some parts and other parts? To what extent does the reader need external information in order to understand it with some adequacy? If he does need more external information, is it the kind of information he could get without undertaking a specialized scholarly inquiry?

3. Analysis can often take the reader's feelings as its point of departure. He may reflect upon his feelings by asking: How does the book (or any of its parts) make me feel? And, why does it make me feel that way? Some books appeal less than others to readers' feelings, but we would find no book interesting unless it moved us. Our purpose is to analyze the book, not ourselves; so we should try to locate the cause of our feelings in the book, not in some peculiarity in ourselves. Once we begin this procedure it is hard to see the end of it, for the effort to account for one's feelings is likely to throw new light on the structure of the book, and this new light will in turn change our feelings. An individual reader's reflections may change frequently like this; and even several centuries of reflection by a succession of readers may follow the same pattern. Why are intelligent readers constantly offering new interpretations of Shakespeare's plays? However satisfactory Johnson's analyses may have been to himself, Coleridge did not seem to think that they accounted for his own feelings (and neither critic thought that his own feelings were peculiar to him), and there are few contemporary readers who think that Coleridge had the last word, even though he may have taught them something about Shakespeare.

The reader's feelings are determined by the kind of person he is, as well as by the structure of the book he reads. One great value of reading good literature lies in the fact that it teaches us what kind of beings we are. By studying the structure of the play we may determine that the death of Cordelia in *King Lear* is a probable consequence of Edmund's plotting; from our response to the scene where Lear weeps over her dead body we may also learn something about our own human nature. Nevertheless, questions about the book itself are the first concern of analytic reading, even when we are analyzing our own feelings. These questions should be

faced before the reader turns to other questions, however legiti-
mate or profound they may be.

4. There are questions the reader might raise about the subject
matter of a book. Thinking of the Roman Empire, as a historical
fact independent of Gibbon's book about it, he might ask: What
does Gibbon omit? Does he stress things that were trivial? Does
he slight things that were important? Questions like these could
also be raised about the problems and ideas of scientific and philosophical books, and even, in a somewhat different way, about the
content of poetic works. But if such questions are raised too soon
they can lead to problems that are indeed interesting, but hard to
answer on first reflection. For example, suppose we ask what parts
of his subject matter an author leaves out, and then apply the question first to a history and then to a play. In general the question can
be answered when it is applied to a history, but not when applied
to a play. (I say in general, because it may indeed be impossible to
answer it with reference to a given history, if that history is our
only available source about that subject; and there have been several plays written about the same subject—for example, about
Oedipus and about Phaedra.) The reader should not too easily
conclude, however, that a great novel is unique and a great history
is not, merely because, with respect to subject matter, novels are
more likely than histories to be unique. Every great book is unique
and it is not easy to say, on first reflection, how its uniqueness is related to its style, its structure, its expressiveness, and its subject.

Chapter 2

History

There are two basic meanings of the term *history:* (1) the past itself, and (2) statements about the past. We are primarily interested in learning to interpret what has been said about the past, in contrast to the professional historian who is more interested in the past itself. The difference is not so sharp as it might seem. We seek to interpret statements about the past, because we want to be able to learn something about the past itself. Conversely, the professional historian cannot learn about the past without working out an intellectual construction; and this intellectual construction must be in some sense a statement.

In interpreting a historical work we must keep in mind that the question of interpretation (understanding what its statements mean) is distinct from the question of truth (how the statements are related to the past), and that the first question is prior. Yet, if we are interpreting the work as history, we must regard our interpretation as somehow incomplete in itself. We cannot be content merely to discover what the statements mean. The very search for their meaning commits us to consider how they could be verified, that is, properly related to the past they refer to. So statements about the past are not independent of the past, when they are interpreted as history.

Much of the past is not independent of what has been said about it. The past is dead, except insofar as it lives in the minds of men, and most of the past can live in men's minds only if it is recorded in writing. This does not mean that nothing at all remains of the past except what men actually remember or have written down. To say this would be like denying that we can ever recall what we have once forgotten. When we recall what we had forgotten, it is usually if not always because some present experience has brought it again to mind. The remembered experience often seems much more or much less important than it did when we actually experienced it. Similarly, some occasion in the present leads the historian, in a sense, to "remind" men of something in the past which they have "forgotten." The event he calls attention to may seem more important now than it did to those who were alive when it happened, or to those who lived in the intervening years. This change is not due to any change in the past itself, or to any change in previously written histories; it is due to changes in the time through which the historian himself is passing.

One might argue that the past lives not only in the minds of men but in the many physical traces it has left. But in traces alone the past is asleep. The historian, not content merely to point to or to collect artifacts or even early writings, insists on doing something to awaken them—to make them more fully alive. He tries to make sense out of them by putting them in intelligible order, by giving them a significance and a place in history. He is satisfied only when he forms a unified construction in his own mind; and if he wishes to communicate this construction to other men, he writes it down. He writes a history.

What the historian writes, then, depends not only on what the past itself was, but on what kind of man the historian is. But conversely what a man is depends very much on what he has learned from the past. When a man of great intelligence becomes interested in the past and writes a history, he is likely to produce a book of lasting value, even though later scholarship may be able to add to what he writes, or even to correct him. This fact bears upon the question, What histories are most appropriate for the general reader?

We can approach the question by considering a paradox. Histories are constantly being rewritten, and yet men continue to read the old superseded histories. Histories are always being rewritten, partly because the past looks different when it is regarded from different points of view, just as a physical object looks different from different perspectives. What we find important in the past depends upon our present interests, and the interests of men are constantly changing. The discovery of new facts also may occasion the writing of new histories. These reasons seem to suggest that the non-historian should read the latest histories and leave the old histories to antiquarians, since the latest histories have the advantage of the most recent discoveries and since their points of view are likely to be closest to that of the reader.

But the fact is that not just antiquarians read the old histories. Continued interest in the writings of Herodotus, Thucydides, Tacitus, and Gibbon testifies to the deep insight these writers had into the past. The past which lives in their books has interested generation after generation of readers and will continue to do so. Our own view of ancient Greece and Rome will be richer if we know how they looked to men of ancient times, or of later times, such as the eighteenth century. Also, for us the old historians are part of history itself. As points of reference, stabilized in space and time, they can help us understand the changes which human attitudes are always undergoing. We would not even know that something was changing, if we could not refer it to something comparatively stable. And for our special purpose, to learn to appreciate and understand written history, it is particularly appropriate to give at least some attention to books which have already proved their lasting value as intelligible works of history.

I

The problems of reading histories can be put into groups which correspond to the two senses of history distinguished at the beginning of this chapter. Since we are primarily concerned with understanding what has been written about the past we shall first turn our attention to reading methods which can help the reader understand just what it is that a history says. In Section II we will consider some of the methods by which the reader can determine whether the history is true.

We shall consider here three basic kinds of questions which should be raised when analyzing histories. The order in which we discuss these questions is not necessarily the order in which they should be asked. The fact is that all three kinds are thoroughly tied up with one another. We must continually move from one to another. An answer to a question of the third sort may arouse new questions of the first or second sort, and so on. In spite of all this there is some reason for raising the questions in the following order: (1) What is the book about? (2) How are its parts inter-related? (3) What is its essential aim, or—more colloquially—what does it all add up to?

The way the book is written may sometimes suggest a different order of raising these questions. The author, for example, fre-quently begins by stating his aims, and questions about aims are questions of the third kind. But it is possible that the author's statement of his aims may actually prove misleading. We are less likely to go wrong if we ask first what kinds of things the author talks about, and we can only know this when we have finished reading the book. This question must surely be answered before we ask how the author relates the various things which he talks about. Only when these two questions are answered can we begin to get a really adequate idea of the author's purpose in writing his book; only then can we evaluate his own statement of his aims.

The Material of Historical Writings

We may think of the material of the historian as analogous to the material out of which any craftsman makes anything, like the bricks of the mason, or the wood of the carpenter. The historian's material is often called *facts*, and facts are of two kinds: (1) events that have happened, and (2) characteristics or qualities. It is not always easy to distinguish between what has happened and the characteristics which tell us what things were like, since we can-not really say what has happened without indicating to some extent what things were like; and one of the best ways to show what things are like is to show what happenings they cause and what happenings they follow from. Nevertheless, it is easy to find illus-trations of writings which are predominantly concerned with one of these kinds of facts or with the other. The *Anglo-Saxon Chroni-*

cle is a clear example of a history with a maximum concern for telling what happened and a minimum concern for characterizing the agents in these happenings. The following passages are typical of the annual entries in the work:

> Anno 409. This year the Goths took the city of Rome by storm, and after this the Romans never ruled in Britain; and this was about eleven hundred and ten years after it had been built. Altogether they ruled in Britain four hundred and seventy years since Caius Julius sought the land.
>
> Anno 418. This year the Romans collected all the treasures that were in Britain, and some they hid in the earth, so that none since has been able to find them; and some they carried with them into Gaul.

In contrast, consider the following passage from Edith Hamilton's *The Greek Way:*

> To rejoice in life, to find the world beautiful and delightful to live in, was a mark of the Greek spirit which distinguished it from all that had gone before. It is a vital distinction. The joy of life is written upon everything the Greeks left behind and they who leave it out of account fail to reckon with something that is of first importance in understanding how the Greek achievement came to pass in the world of antiquity. It is not a fact that jumps to the eye for the reason that their literature is marked as strongly by sorrow. The Greeks knew to the full how bitter life is as well as how sweet. Joy and sorrow, exultation and tragedy, stand hand in hand in Greek literature, but there is no contradiction involved thereby. Those who do not know the one do not really know the other either. It is the depressed, the gray-minded people, who cannot rejoice just as they cannot agonize. The Greeks were not the victims of depression. Greek literature is not done in gray or with a low palette. It is all black and shining white or black and scarlet and gold. The Greeks were keenly aware, terribly aware, of life's uncertainty and the imminence of death. Over and over again they emphasize the brevity and the failure of all human endeavor, the swift passing of all that is beautiful and joyful. To Pindar, even as he glorifies the victor in the games, life is "a shadow's dream." But never, not in their darkest moments, do they lose their taste for

life. It is always a wonder and a delight, the world a place of beauty, and they themselves rejoicing to be alive in it.[1]

This passage attempts to give a picture of the ancient "Greek spirit." It is not concerned with "happenings"; it tells no narrative. We must not fail to notice, however, that the spirit which is the subject of this description is, in a sense, placed in a sequence. The author distinguishes it "from all that had gone before." Consider also the title of the book, and another passage:

None of the great civilizations that preceded them served them as model. With them something completely new came into the world. They were the first Westerners; the spirit of the West, the modern spirit, is a Greek discovery and the place of the Greeks is in the modern world.[2]

It is clear that Miss Hamilton is not reconstructing the Greek spirit for its own sake, but showing how it led to the modern spirit. This should remind us that the distinction between narrative and descriptive history is not hard and fast and that our interest in histories, narrative or descriptive, is never detached from our interest in the present. In a basic sense all histories are narrative; the mere fact that history is concerned with the past means that when we study any part of it we give it a place in a time sequence. Nevertheless, the distinction is useful, and the reader should try to determine the different degrees of importance which historians give to narrative or to descriptive elements. Otherwise he might, for personal reasons, attribute more importance to a given fact than the historian wants him to, and thus misunderstand what he reads.

Some illustrations may help to show how histories differ in immediate subject matter, and in relating different kinds of subjects to one another. These illustrations may also suggest how questions about subject matter can lead the reader to questions about the organization of the material and about the purposes of the historian.

In the opening lines of his *History* Herodotus says that he writes

---

[1] Edith Hamilton, *The Greek Way* (New York: W. W. Norton & Co., 1930), pp. 32–33.
[2] *Ibid.*, p. 19.

in order to preserve from decay "the remembrance of what men have done" and "to prevent the great and wonderful deeds of the Greeks and the Barbarians from losing their due meed of glory." "What men have done" and "wonderful deeds" indicate the primary role we may expect overt actions to play in his work. This expectation is borne out when he goes on to say: "According to the Persians best informed in history, the Phoenicians began the quarrel." His book is evidently a narrative of memorable conflicts between Greeks and non-Greeks, and the descriptive matter he includes—and there is much of it—helps to make clear the nature and importance of the deeds which he relates.

Many of the facts in Edward Gibbon's *Decline and Fall of the Roman Empire* could scarcely have been included in order to reflect glory upon anyone, and Gibbon does not seem to be worried about "the remembrance of what men have done." In the course of his narrative he says much about the personal character of many emperors, in particular about the character of "bad" emperors. The reader might think that some of the things he tells us about Commodus, for example, ought to have been forgotten. But Herodotus and Gibbon select their facts for different reasons, as the reader should suspect when he notices these factual differences. It is not a morbid interest in depravity that leads Gibbon to tell us the sordid facts about Commodus, but their bearing upon a different kind of fact, which greatly interests Gibbon: the political structure of the Roman Empire. The following passage shows how important Gibbon thought the emperor was in this structure, and it also suggests something about the central importance of that political structure in Gibbon's view of his subject, the decline and fall of an empire:

> The labours of these monarchs were overpaid by the immense reward that inseparably waited on their success; by the honest pride of virtue, and by the exquisite delight of beholding the general happiness of which they were the authors. A just but melancholy reflection embittered, however, the noblest of human enjoyments. They must often have recollected the instability of a happiness which depended upon the character of a single man. The

16

fatal moment was perhaps approaching when some licentious youth or some jealous tyrant would abuse, to the destruction, that absolute power which they had exerted for the benefit, of their people. The ideal restraints of the senate and the laws might serve to display the virtues, but could never correct the vices, of the emperor. The military force was a blind and irresistible instrument of oppression; and the corruption of Roman manners would always supply flatterers eager to applaud, and ministers prepared to serve, the fear or the avarice, the lust or the cruelty, of their masters.[3]

This passage also illustrates the close interdependence possible between narrative and descriptive passages in histories. It is clearly a descriptive passage, but we hardly need to look beyond the passage itself to see that the author intends it to explain a narrative of events. This is borne out by the succeeding chapters, which begin with an account of a "licentious youth and jealous tyrant," Commodus, and go on to trace in chronological order the stages in the fall of the empire. As the narrative unfolds, the facts which most interest Gibbon seem to be the changes in the state of the empire brought about by the shifts of power among the various elements of the Roman Empire—the constitution, the emperor, the army, the senate, and the people.

The facts which are elements of narratives are often called *events*. What constitutes an event in a history depends upon the scope of the history. In a broad universal history the American Civil War might be an event; but in a history of that war an event might rather be the battle of Gettysburg, or even the charge of Pickett's brigade, or Lincoln's Gettysburg address. Each of these things happened, and each has a completeness of its own, although they differ in magnitude. The importance an author gives to a detail like Pickett's charge may, of course, also tell us something about the nature and scope of the historian's aims. The *Anglo-Saxon Chronicle* illustrates this point. It treats the battle of Brunanburgh in greater detail than it does the storming of Rome, which is only surprising if we fail to realize that the *Chronicle* is a Saxon

---

[3] Edward Gibbon, *The Decline and Fall of the Roman Empire*, Modern Library ed. (New York, 1932), I, 70.

history and therefore the comparative importance of the two events is determined by the particular interests of the Saxons.

If we consider several histories of approximately the same scope, the different aspects which they may stress will suggest other ways of distinguishing kinds of events. A history of World War II might stress the physical clashes involved in actual military operations; the economic developments which affected the willingness and ability of one side or another to wage war; the technological developments which helped to determine the effectiveness of fighting forces on land, sea, and air; the formulation of scientific theories responsible for the development of these technologies; the rhetorical arguments which moved men to undertake scientific inquiries; the technological application of scientific theories; the military employment of technological products; and so on. The dropping of a bomb is an event, and so is its manufacture, its engineering, the theorizing which makes its engineering possible, and a speech advocating its use. Any aspect of human activity, thought, or emotion may be regarded as an event. Any one or several of these may be more or less stressed or ignored by any given historian.

These distinctions among kinds of events suggest even further differences among historians. There might be agreement that the conference of Roosevelt, Churchill, and Stalin at Yalta was an event, and, in treating this, several historians might be said to be pointing to the same thing. But mere pointing does not tell us precisely what the pointer wishes to call attention to. One historian might think of the Yalta conference as a meeting of powerful political personalities, and the other might think of it as a conference of sovereign nations for whom Roosevelt, Churchill, and Stalin were merely spokesmen. Also, if different evidence about the same event is available to several historians, the event will not really be the same for each of them. Even if the evidence seems to be the same, different interpretations of that evidence will change the character of the event. The forces back of a great movement like the Crusades may seem to some writers predominantly economic; to others, political; and to still others, religious.

The characteristics and qualities which make up part of the

material of histories can be as varied as events. A nation may be characterized by its economy, its political structure, its fine and industrial arts, or even its geographical situation. An author may tell us explicitly what sort of characteristics he regards as relevant or irrelevant. Henry Osborn Taylor warns, "We must not drift too far with studies of daily life, habits and dress, wars and raiding, crimes and brutalities, or trade and craft and agriculture."[4] The title of Taylor's book, *The Mediaeval Mind*, itself suggests the sort of characteristics which would be relevant facts for him; the reader of history will not always find such explicit guidance and must be alert to notice the sorts of characteristics included or left out and on which the stress is placed. Another sentence from the same book may serve to remind us of the close interconnection between events and characteristics: "If we would attain . . . an orderly presentation of mediaeval intellectual and emotional development, we must avoid entanglements with manifold and not always relevant detail."[5] This tells us that Taylor is concerned with a development, and therefore with something which is in a sense a narrative; and also, that his particular "narrative" purpose is what compels him to select only certain characteristics as relevant for his purpose.

At the beginning of this section we spoke of facts as the material of histories. We have been speaking of two basic kinds of facts, events and characteristics and have treated them as elements whose occurrence or existence is thought to be established. Some facts can be more directly established than others. The moral and intellectual characteristics of individual men, and certainly of whole peoples, cannot be directly established but must be inferred from the way people behave. Visible objects, on the other hand, can sometimes be directly observed, even though there are times when they can be established only by inference. If we find the bodies of dead soldiers on the battlefield, we may reasonably infer that they were killed in action. If, however, we wish to know whether

---

[4] *The Mediaeval Mind* (4th ed.; London: Macmillan & Co., 1938), I, xii.
[5] *Ibid.*

the soldiers died bravely, we must resort to inference, even if a surviving witness saw them die. Awareness of this distinction not only can help the reader judge the accuracy of a historian's account; it can also help him notice the kind of material which particularly interests the historian.

Principles of Relationship in Historical Writings

A well-written history is more than a mere collection of facts. A historian makes his work more than a collection by relating facts to one another. The facts of history may be related to one another because they are all connected with the same subject. We can begin to grasp the formal unity of a history if we can sharply define its subject—if, that is, we can say what it is that the history is a history of. The subject may be a substance (a man, a building, a document) or an action (a journey, or a war) or a place (London, or England, considered as geographical entities) or an institution (the Congress of the United States), and so on.

The reader's grasp of the formal unity of a history can be made more precise if he is able to determine the separate parts into which the history divides its subject; these subdivisions may or may not be explicitly stated. The reader should find the principle or principles according to which the subject has been subdivided. A history of Europe might be divided according to geographical or political units, or according to topics such as wars, economic developments, and religious movements. The reader should ask why the historian divides his subject as he does (why he uses temporal, geographical, or certain topical principles) and why he draws his dividing lines where he does (why, for instance, at 1700, rather than at 1650 or 1750).

If the material of a history consists chiefly of events, these events may be interrelated as the parts of a novel or play may be interrelated, because all such works are fundamentally narrative in structure. The history may have an action like the plot of a novel. The actions of histories and the plots of novels and plays all have settings and involve character and thought. (These structural elements receive more detailed treatment in the chapter on the interpretation of drama and fiction.) The action of a history, like the plot of a novel, may develop along one or along several lines of action. If there are several, the lines may diverge (as the growth of the British people led to the development of the separate nations of the United States, Canada, Australia) or they may converge (as the establishment of several colonies led ultimately to the development of a single nation, the United States).

If the material of a history consists chiefly of characteristics or qualities, these need not be placed in a narrative sequence but may be differentiated and classified. The reader should notice how the characteristics or qualities are differentiated or grouped and should try to find the bases for these differentiations and groupings. He should also try to account for the order in which these elements are taken up.

It is most characteristically historical to relate facts to one another in a temporal order. We have seen that the formal unity of a history can be partially grasped if we can define its subject, and more precisely grasped if we can understand the division of this subject into parts. Most historians are not content merely to relate the parts of their subject to one another; they seek to explain precisely *why* a given event follows from certain past events and leads to certain later events. And the stressing of causes differs, in both kind and degree, from one historian to another.

There are probably no histories which try to explain everything. Sometimes no more than the temporal order of things is set down. There may be a number of reasons for this, and the reader should ask what these might be. Does the author think no explanation is needed or does he think none is possible? It is probably one or the other of these reasons, in some form. The sort of explanation an event may need depends in part on how familiar that sort of event is. History records innumerable human births and deaths, but these phenomena are so familiar to us that we do not demand explanations of them. We may be so well satisfied with our understanding of the way certain things happen that we accept a statement of a fact without inquiring further into it. If we are told that Julius Caesar died when he was stabbed, we think we understand well enough the connection between stabbing and death. It is more important to realize that the sort of explanation required may be determined by the scope and purpose of the particular history. In one history it may be sufficient to say that Lincoln was elected President in 1860, but in another the steps leading up to this event may need to be covered in great detail. Such differences suggest that the two histories' essential purposes are very different.

A writer may fail to offer an explanation of an event because he cannot find one or because the event was caused by chance, so to speak, or because its explanation merely happens to be hidden. What we call an accident does to a certain extent defy explanation. Sometimes the simple statement, "It was an accident," is the only explanation possible. There are other things which we can usually explain, but whose explanation escapes us in a particular instance. We can explain death by saying that a man died of disease, by violence, suicide, old age, or accident; but in a particular instance we may not be able to determine what caused death. All of this is greatly complicated by the fact that a great many influences have a bearing upon the occurrence of any event. Public officials or insurance companies are not always content to call an event simply an accident. The occurrence of an automobile crash is certainly accidental, but a number of things had to coincide before it could happen. An investigation may conclude that one of the drivers did not obey traffic laws, or that the road or a car's brakes were faulty. The histories produced by such investigations suggest that any given history does not simply explain or not explain. Analysis should help the reader unravel the complexities which historians deal with and make him more aware of the pattern of interrelationships which a historian constructs, the pattern which makes his writing a unified work instead of a collection of fragments.

We have been concerned with the extent to which a historian may explain the facts in his history (and it is by explanations that he relates the facts to one another). We should also raise questions about the kinds of explanations he offers.

The range of possible explanations can be suggested by imagining an historical work on the causes of the outbreak of war between the United States and the Japanese Empire in December, 1941. The historian may seek to determine what action precipitated the war, what agency performed this action, what motives led this agency to do it, what situations produced these motives, what in turn produced these situations and so on. We must remember such questions cannot be answered neatly and simply, one by one, because they cut across each other in very complex ways.

It may be helpful to raise questions a reader might ask about the different kinds of causes outlined above. Even if one or more of them is unimportant in any given history, this negative fact will help us to understand that history.

First, was the action which precipitated the war between Japan and the United States the attack on Pearl Harbor on December 7, 1941, or was it President Roosevelt's address to Congress on December 8, 1941? Whatever the immediate occasion of the war may have been, historians are fond of asking, What was the *real* cause? Some historians would say that the real cause of this war was a large-scale conflict between fascism and democracy, or between German, Italian, and Japanese imperialism, on the one hand, and British and American imperialism, on the other hand.

Questions about the action which caused the war are obviously tied up with questions about the agency responsible for it. The agent might be said to be a person, like Tojo or Hitler; a political party, like the "militarist" party of Tojo; a nation, like Japan or Germany; or something even more general and abstract, like the "spirit" of an age.

If we ask why the agency did what it did, the answers may again be infinitely various. A man or a nation may be said to act for economic, political, or ideological motives. These motives themselves may be explained by reference to the character of a man, or even of a people, or by reference to what has been done to this man or this people. These explanations are bound up with psychological, economic, political, or philosophical doctrines of all kinds, and it is hard to conceive of any point at which further questions could not be raised.

For some historians the questions, Who did it? or, What were his motives? are unimportant; they are interested in finding answers to more ultimate questions, such as, Is there a logic of history? In the *Decline of the West*, for example, Oswald Spengler says:

> In this book is attempted for the first time the venture of predetermining history, of following the still unravelled stages in the destiny of a Culture, and specifically of the only Culture of our time and on our planet which is actually in the phase of fulfilment —the West-European–American. . . .
>
> Is there a logic of history? Is there, beyond all the casual and incalculable elements of the separate events, something that we may call the metaphysical structure of historic humanity, something that is essentially independent of the outward forms—social, spiritual and political—which we see so clearly? Are not these actualities indeed secondary or derived from that something? Does world-history present to the seeing eye certain grand traits, again and again, with sufficient constancy to justify certain conclusions? And if so, what are the limits to which reasoning from such premises may be pushed?[6]

Spengler thought he had discovered, by studying history, a "logic of history," a "metaphysical structure of historic humanity." He believed that if certain agents with certain motives had not in fact appeared on the stage of history, others would have taken their place and the course of history would have been substantially the same. So confident was he of this that he thought he could predict future history, since its course would not depend, according to his view, upon the appearance of particular men like Tojo, Hitler, Churchill, Roosevelt, or Stalin.

There are historians who, although they do not, like Spengler, venture to predict coming events, do stress the power of some

---

[6] Oswald Spengler, *The Decline of the West*, trans. C. F. Atkinson (Special ed.; New York: Alfred A. Knopf, 1939), I, 3.

ultimate cause largely independent of the actions and motives of particular men or particular peoples. This ultimate cause has sometimes been thought of as supernatural, as Destiny or God. The ultimate cause of historical events has been located in natural processes connected, for example, with the growth of population and the necessary conditions of life. Some of these principles have been summarized by Charles and Mary Beard:

> It was not without some warrant, perhaps, that one of the very earliest Greek Philosophers, Anaximander, more than five centuries before the Christian era, reached the startling conclusion that the cosmos which he beheld with penetrating eyes was a limitless flood, ever in motion, throwing up new forms and beings and drawing them again into its devouring immensity according to the law of destiny—whirling worlds, swaying tides, growing crops, wandering herds, puny man, and his little systems erected proudly for a day against eternity being but symbols of an unchanging force, the essence of all reality. Conceived even in terms of modern mathematics, a purely mechanistic philosophy is engaging in its simplicity, but we are warned by one recent historian, Henry Adams, that mere motion cannot account for direction or for the problems of vital energy; and by another, Oswald Spengler, that "there is an organic logic, an instinctive, dream-sure logic of all existence, as opposed to the logic of the inorganic, the logic of understanding and of things understood—a logic of direction as against a logic of extension.
>
> More than two thousand years after Anaximander, in the nineteenth century, the German philosopher, Hegel, seeking the solution to the endless changes of history, came to the conclusion that the evolution of humanity was, in its inmost nature, the progressive revelation of the divine spirit. Assuming, as necessary, God the unconditioned, creator and upholder of all, Hegel saw in the kaleidoscopic time-patterns of civilization, strewn through the ages, mere partial reflections of the grand idea underlying the universe—"an infinite power realizing its aim in the absolute rational design of the world." Nations rising and declining were to him but pawns in a majestic game, each with its mission to fulfill, with its heroes as servants of their epochs carrying out that aspect of the Idea then fated for realization.

Near the close of Hegel's century, a German economist. Werner Sombart, seeking the dynamic of imperialism, reduced the process to the terms of an everlasting struggle among human societies over feeding places on the wide surface of the earth and over the distribution of the world's natural resources.[7]

No matter what his view of causation, the historian may not feel the need of explaining events by reference to a single ultimate cause, or to a well-defined order of many causes. Even if a person thinks that a complicated machine works according to the plan of its engineer, he might concern himself, in writing an account of the workings of the machine, with a detailed description of the mechanical linkages which transmit power from its source throughout the cycle of the machine's operation. In the same way, if the historian thinks history is determined by Fate, he may still explain events by reference to human motives, cleverness, or carelessness, and to natural occurrences like earthquakes or storms. Herodotus assigns significant roles in Croesus' downfall to the decree of the Fates against him (pronounced many generations before his birth), to his ancestor who provoked the Fates into making the decree, to the military skill of Croesus' enemy Cyrus, to the characters of the Lydians and the Persians, to the fact that a precipice which stood at one edge of Sardis was left undefended, and to Croesus' pride. Even if the decree of the Fates was thought to be inexorable, this does not prevent Herodotus from narrating the story as though much depended upon the Persians' decision to enter Sardis by way of the undefended precipice.

Whenever we pause in the infinite process of raising more and more questions to answer the latest one, that answer may throw a different light on earlier questions. This is one reason why a book can look so different when we read it for a second time. I do not mean to suggest that the order in which I have mentioned possible questions is the order in which the historian has written his book. I suggest only a general framework of questions, and their order should be regarded as flexible. If, early in our analysis, we read that

---

[7] *The Rise of American Civilization* (New York: Macmillan Co., 1927), I, 4-5.

the war with Japan was caused by the attack on Pearl Harbor, the real nature of that attack may become much clearer to us after we have carried our analysis much further and have understood its larger context.

Just as a later question about causes may throw light on an earlier question about causes, so the whole series of questions about the interrelations of historical facts may throw light on questions about the facts themselves. We cannot get very far in describing or defining anything without showing how it is related to other things, how it follows from some of them, and how it leads to others.

The Aims of Historical Writings

The opening paragraphs of many histories include explicit statements of their writers' aims. We must not, of course, disregard these explicit statements, but we must be careful not to attribute too much significance to them. They may not really tell us much about the ultimate aims of their authors; often they tell us only the kind of material the authors will be concerned with, not the reason for their concern with it. Take, for example, this sentence from the first paragraph of Gibbon's *Decline and Fall of the Roman Empire:*

> It is the design of this, and of the two succeeding chapters, to describe the prosperous condition of their empire; and afterwards, from the death of Marcus Antoninus, to deduce the most important circumstances of its decline and fall: a revolution which will ever be remembered, and is still felt by the nations of the earth.

The reader will not be able to state Gibbon's real aims until he can say what Gibbon thought "the most important circumstances" were, why he thought they were important, and how he thought they were to be "deduced."

Where historians do not give explicit statements of their aims it is not easy to determine what they are. Experienced readers, however, know that, although there are as many historical aims as there are histories, both aims and histories can be grouped into kinds. We may begin with a distinction which is useful in the interpretation of historical literature, although impossible to find perfectly exemplified.

A writer's aim may be what we shall call "purely historical," or "extra-historical." The writer whose aim is purely historical is interested only in telling what happened; he has no further aim. The writer with an extra-historical aim has an extra-historical reason for what he says, a reason beyond the desire simply to tell what happened. The reason it is impossible to find the distinction perfectly exemplified is that "pure" history is, strictly speaking, impossible, for it suggests an interest that is completely independent of other interests. A writer is a man before he is a historian, and the particular historical problems that interest him are determined by the kind of man he is. We can nevertheless say that some writers, more than others, subordinate their other interests to their interest in determining and explaining historical facts.

Extra-historical aims. We shall distinguish three kinds of extra-historical aims: (*a*) poetic, (*b*) rhetorical, and (*c*) scientific. It is important for us to distinguish these from purely historical aims, because there is a large quantity of important poetic, rhetorical, and scientific literature that uses historical material. In addition to many classical works of this kind, newspapers and news magazines are historical writings, and they very frequently select the news they publish, and employ particular manners of reporting, because their publishers are motivated by extra-historical aims— they are not always primarily interested in helping the public to understand what has happened. The poetic and rhetorical aims of some historical writings could have been treated in chapters 3 and 5, on drama and fiction and on rhetoric. Scientific aims could perhaps have been treated in the discussion of philosophy in chapter 4. This consideration may remind us that the distinctions expressed in the chapter titles of this book are not intended to suggest that any given work can be neatly placed in one category or another. And I hope it may comfort any readers who find it disturbing to consider such works as Shakespeare's historical plays under the rubric of history. Writings with extra-historical aims are difficult to classify; but they are a large part of an intelligent reader's experience, and they present special problems of interpretation.

Just as some writers are more purely historical than others, it can be said that in general (and there are many important exceptions to this generalization) "poetic" history is most remote from, and "scientific" history closest to, "pure" history. For this reason we shall consider extra-historical aims in the order that has been given.

When a writer, say, of a narrative history, has a special interest in the mere telling of his story, he has what we are calling a *poetic aim*, and we shall use the term *poetic* broadly enough to include drama and fiction, as well as lyric poetry. What is meant will be clearer if we imagine an extreme case, a writer so much interested in the telling of his story that he freely alters the facts in order to make the story better. Short of this extreme we can allow a historian to arrange his facts dramatically, if we do not suspect him of altering the facts, or of oversimplifying their relationships. A writer like this may certainly be a genuine historian, motivated though he is in part by poetic aims.

Famous historians are often accused of using history as a mere framework upon which to place interesting tales, striking aphorisms, or witticisms. It is said, for example, that the story about the phoenix, and others like it, in the second book of Herodotus is included in the history merely because Herodotus loved a good story. Some also say that Gibbon used the history of Rome as an opportunity for stringing together a series of well-turned phrases flavored with ironic wit. It is all right to be alert to the possibility that any given writer may be turning history into some kind of poetry—dramatic, epic, fictional, or lyric—but the reader should not jump to conclusions too quickly. These poetic elements need not be incompatible with historical purposes. That people believed the story of the phoenix burying its parents may be historically true and important. Actual historical occurrences may have many of the same qualities which writers of fiction love; in fact, if they did not have some of these qualities historians might ignore them.

Again, wit and irony, which are enjoyable in themselves, may subserve strictly historical purposes; they may be the best means the historian has of calling attention to the things he considers historically important.

A reader may easily, while he is reading a history, find himself taking the attitude of a reader of fiction, and vice versa. It may be that the most effective means of preventing this, in a history, is to ask the question, Is it true? This question will be the subject of the last part of this chapter. But even before this question is raised, the historical attitude may be maintained by asking continually, Does the author *assert* this to be historically true? It is often very difficult to answer this question, because the intentions of good authors are not simple in this respect.

Consider the historical plays of Shakespeare. They are certainly histories of a sort, and are more "historical" than many books we call "historical novels." Richard II, Richard III, and Henry IV actually lived and ruled, and there is good evidence that Shakespeare's portrayals of them have some historical foundation. Some events in the plays are not very certain historically, and others, like Henry IV's famous soliloquy on sleep, are clearly not intended to be literal accounts of what actually happened. This soliloquy runs as follows, in King Henry IV's words:

> How many thousand of my poorest subjects
> Are at this hour asleep! O Sleep, O gentle Sleep,
> Nature's soft nurse, how have I frighted thee
> That thou no more wilt weigh my eyelids down
> And steep my senses in forgetfulness?
> Why rather, Sleep, liest thou in smoky cribs,
> Upon uneasy pallets stretching thee,
> And hush'd with buzzing night-flies to thy slumber,
> Than in the perfum'd chambers of the great
> Under the canopies of costly state,
> And lull'd with sound of sweetest melody?[8]

Now, Shakespeare would not have us believe that King Henry IV ever said precisely these words. But even a writer like Thucydides,

---

[8] 2 Henry IV, Act III, sc. 1, lines 4–14.

who is more clearly a historian and not a dramatic poet, does not claim that the speeches he records were ever given in the words he sets down:

> With reference to the speeches in this history, some were delivered before the war began, others while it was going on; some I heard myself, others I got from various quarters; it was in all cases difficult to carry them word for word in one's memory, so my habit has been to make the speakers say what was in my opinion demanded of them by the various occasions, of course adhering as closely as possible to the general sense of what they really said.[9]

There are clear differences here between Shakespeare and Thucydides. Thucydides does claim that, for every speech he records, a speech corresponding to it was actually given and that the recorded speech adheres closely to the general sense of what was really said. Shakespeare makes neither of these claims. Furthermore, Pericles might well have said something very like the words Thucydides gives him, but Henry IV could not possibly have spoken Shakespeare's lines. These lines are poetry which no one but Shakespeare could have written. How should the reader regard them? It would surely be absurd to chop the plays up into parts and say, "I will read this part as history, and that part as poetry." This would have the effect of making the same character, Henry IV, be two different characters, one historical and the other poetic. As a result the book would tend to become unintelligible. It seems clear that, whatever Shakespeare intended his book to be, the character of Henry IV is intended to be one character; the play falls apart unless it is so understood. *Henry IV*, is not simply a history nor is it simply dramatic poetry; but its structure is determined in part by poetic aims.

In general, any book whose organization is primarily determined by poetic principles, and which successfully carries out its aims, can be understood as poetry and need arouse no peculiarly historical questions in the reader's mind.

The reader should try to determine how far poetic aims have

---

[9] *The Complete Writings of Thucydides,* Modern Library ed. (New York, 1934), p. 14.

affected what the writer says. It is possible for them to affect it so far that the book loses its essentially historical character. On the other hand, they may do no more than put facts together in an intelligible order; for example, they may make a sequence of historical events understandable as a narrative. Between these extremes there are many roles which poetic aims can play in the construction of histories. The reader should learn to notice the presence of these aims, and to judge the extent of their influence.

In turning to the consideration of *rhetorical aims*, we must keep in mind that no one writes a history, or any other book for that matter, without hoping to affect his readers in certain ways. Even a "purely scientific" writer hopes to change his readers' minds, and the way he writes is controlled, in part, by that hope. If we think of rhetoric as that aspect of writing which is particularly concerned with making an effect upon readers' minds or improving communication between the author and the reader, we shall see that writings which have poetic and scientific aims can also have rhetorical aims.

We are not now concerned with the aim of improving communication between writer and reader, but with the aim of persuading the reader to act or be disposed to act in a certain way. Works (or passages of works) may have such an aim and may seek to achieve it by appealing to examples from history. A passage from Thomas Carlyle's *The French Revolution* exemplifies this:

> Wherefore let all men know what of depth and of height is still revealed in man; and with fear and wonder, with just sympathy and just antipathy, with clear eye and open heart, contemplate it and appropriate it; and draw innumerable inferences from it. This inference, for example, among the first: That 'if the gods of this lower world will sit on their glittering thrones, indolent as Epicurus' gods, with the living Chaos of Ignorance and Hunger weltering uncared-for at their feet, and smooth Parasites preaching Peace, peace, when there is no peace,' then the dark Chaos, it would seem will rise;—has risen, and, O Heavens! has it not tanned their skins into breeches for itself? That there be no second Sansculottism in our Earth for a thousand years, let us under-

stand well what the first was; and let Rich and Poor of us go and do *otherwise*.[10]

Carlyle wants to persuade men not to behave in certain ways, and bases his effort on an appeal to the way two classes of people behaved during the French Revolution. The selection is only a fragment of his book, but it should be noted that his appeal (to the rich and poor of a thousand years) is based on his account of a single revolution. This fact indicates a difference between rhetorical and scientific aims. In historical writing a rhetorical aim is characteristically sought by means of a small number of striking examples, which are hardly enough to establish a *theory* about human behavior, and it is theories of this sort that histories with scientific aims seek to establish.

His interest in a small number of striking examples helps to account for the vividness of Carlyle's language. He cannot be content merely to refer to the historical example. He must intensify its effect by poetic means—he uses figures of speech which help to make his language eloquent (calling the French nobility "the gods of this lower world," and the masses who revolted "the dark Chaos"). The reader's alertness to the use of such poetic devices can help him understand the manner in which a historical work should be interpreted. He should try to determine the extent to which this or any other extra-historical feature affects the structure of the book. Whether or not the writer's view of the facts is distorted by extra-historical aims, failure to notice them can result in misinterpretation.

Historical writings with *scientific aims* deal, for the most part, with materials appropriate for the social sciences. It is easy to see how "natural history" can be the basis of theories of natural science. Geology and paleontology are in large part studies of the past, and their historical aspects have been useful in establishing modern scientific theories. The study and the historical dating of the existence of certain animals has led to the formulation of extremely general theories of biology. Similarly, the study of actual

---

[10] Modern Library ed. (New York, 1934), p. 719.

economic or political changes may advance our knowledge of economic or political theory, and of ethics. R. H. Tawney's *Religion and the Rise of Capitalism* claims by its very title to be something more than historical, something general and theoretical. Tawney also calls it "A Historical Study." Its opening sentence is a good example of an explicit statement of aims which really does no more than call attention to the book's subject:

> The object of this book is to trace some strands in the development of religious thought on social and economic questions in the period which saw the transition from medieval to modern theories of social organization.[11]

We have already noticed how the title of the book suggests something more about Tawney's purpose. The epigraph, a quotation from Berkeley's *Siris* suggests still more:

> Whatever the world thinks, he who hath not much meditated upon God, the human mind, and the *summum bonum*, may possibly make a thriving earthworm, but will most indubitably make a sorry patriot and a sorry statesman.

An epigraph often suggests the theme of a book, and this epigraph is a generalization of a political, even of a moral, sort.

It is not easy to determine Tawney's real aim, but the difficulty of the problem makes his book worthy of further analysis along this line. At the beginning of his first chapter Tawney attempts to defend the importance of his study:

> The attempt to judge economic activity and social organization by ethical criteria raises problems which are eternal, and it is possible that a study of the thought of an age when that attempt was made, if with little success, at least with conviction and persistence, may prove, even today, not wholly without instruction.[12]

The upshot of this is that "the object of this book" which was stated in the first sentence, quoted above, and which seems strictly

---

[11] R. H. Tawney, *Religion and the Rise of Capitalism*, New American Library (New York, 1947), p. 1.

[12] *Ibid.*, p. 11.

historical, can itself be pursued for the sake of a further object: the solution of eternal problems which are not historical in character. Some of Tawney's remarks encourage the reader to think that the book is concerned with the history of one of these "eternal problems" and not necessarily with establishing the truth or falsity of any proposed solutions to these problems. In speaking of "the doctrine that religion and economic interests form two separate and co-ordinate kingdoms, of which neither, without presumption, can encroach on the other," he says, "A historian is concerned less to appraise the validity of an idea than to understand its development."[13] This seems like a clear case of separating the strictly historical aim from an extra-historical aim, but the reader should not conclude too quickly that Tawney is not concerned with appraising the validity of this idea (which he himself recognizes as less historical than understanding its development). The reader will find many reasons for suspecting that Tawney is very much concerned with the validity of this and other ideas whose history he traces. Tawney's last chapter contains several passages like the following:

> The certainties of one age are the problems of the next. Few will refuse their admiration to the magnificent conception of a community penetrated from apex to foundation by the moral law, which was the inspiration of the great reformers, not less than of the better minds of the Middle Ages. But, in order to subdue the tough world of material interests, it is necessary to have at least so much sympathy with its tortuous ways as is needed to understand them. The Prince of Darkness has a right to a courteous hearing and a fair trial, and those who will not give him his due are wont to find that, in the long run, he turns the tables by taking his due and something over. Common sense and a respect for realities are not less graces of the spirit than moral zeal.
> . . . If, however, economic ambitions are good servants, they are bad masters. Harnessed to a social purpose, they will turn the mill and grind the corn. But the question, to what end the wheels revolve, still remains; and on that question the naive and uncritical

---

[13] *Ibid.*, p. 4.

worship of economic power, which is the mood of unreason too often engendered in those whom that new Leviathan has hypnotized by its spell, throws no light. Its result is not seldom a world in which men command a mechanism that they cannot fully use, and an organization which has every perfection except that of motion.[14]

Much of this is written in the present tense, and is in very general terms. True, the title of this chapter is "Conclusion," but the conclusion is the conclusion of a historical study; that is, it seems clear that Tawney believes he has in some sense demonstrated his conclusion, and demonstrated it historically.

The importance of historical studies for the social sciences is hard to exaggerate, if we allow our conception of history to include what happened yesterday, or this morning. The social scientist is much less able than the natural scientist to experiment with his subject matter, and must in his researches rely heavily upon historical knowledge of what men have done in various social circumstances. I suggest that Tawney, on the basis of historical studies, moves toward conclusions that might well belong to the sciences of economics or political economy, or to a branch of moral theory. Tawney's whole book would have to be studied before this interpretation could be accepted or rejected.

Even if Tawney is pursuing an extra-historical aim he need not necessarily be incapable of pursuing the strictly historical aim: giving an account of what actually happened in the past. Some ulterior aims are more likely than others to distort our views. We are in general least likely to distort facts which bear upon theories of natural science, and most likely to distort those which bear upon things that affect our personal interests. Economic, political, or moral theories probably occupy a middle ground.

Purely historical aims. The historian's purely historical aim is to put forward a historical thesis. A simple assertion like "Columbus discovered America" is a historical thesis. Or a thesis may be much more complex, like the Marxist view of history as a class struggle.

---

[14] *Ibid.*, pp. 231–32.

Some, like "There actually was a King Arthur," assert the existence of something; others, like "Adolf Hitler is dead," assert the non-existence of something. Some assert that a given subject has a certain quality: "Cleopatra was a beautiful woman." Some assert a causal connection between things: "The American Colonies declared their independence because they resented taxation without representation." Theses may concern different kinds of subjects. The subject may be a specific person or thing, like Socrates or the Parthenon; it may be an individual in a special sense, like "The Man of the Renaissance," or "the United States Steel Corporation"; it may be collective, like the mob attacking the Bastille; it may be an institution, like the American presidency, or the collective group of individual men who make that institution real, the American presidents.

Theses may attribute different kinds of actions or characteristics to their subjects. These may be single actions, "Caesar invaded Britain"; or repeated actions, "The Danes harried the English coast whenever and wherever vigilance relaxed"; or continuous actions, "Throughout the fifth century the barbarians pressed against the frontiers of the Empire." They may represent something as beginning, developing, or ending, "The Germans began submarine attacks off the Atlantic coast in 1941, submarine warfare reached its peak in 1943, and submarine warfare was no longer an important factor after 1944." These examples by no means exhaust the possibilities and are meant only to be suggestive. They are not intended to encourage the student to fit works into neat categories, but rather to stimulate his search for the main thesis or theses of the history he is reading.

A thesis, even for a long book, may sometimes be stated comparatively briefly. The reader should try to summarize the thesis, but he should be cautious; to discuss one's hypotheses with other readers of the book is a valuable aid to the development of care in this reading skill, as well as in others. A large history of Rome might be said to have the thesis that Rome fell because of the growth of Christianity. The unity of the entire book might here be explained by showing how each part of the book is related to this central thesis. It could also be, however, that an accurate statement of this book's thesis would require a fairly long synopsis of the events recounted in the history. Such a thesis might be stated in a long compound sentence: "This happened, and then that happened, because this also happened, while these other things were going on." Hypotheses which differ so radically should be tested against one another both to prevent oversimplification, on the one hand, and, on the other, to keep the reader from getting lost in a mass of details, from failing to see the forest for the trees.

The reader of a history should first try to understand what that history asserts. He may then go on to ask whether the assertion is true. In general this second question belongs to a critical level of reading and is more appropriate for the reader who wishes to learn what really happened than for the reader who wishes merely to learn the meaning of what is said about the past. It might seem that the latter need not even raise the question, Is it true? But it should be apparent by now that reading cannot be genuinely historical if this question is totally absent from the mind. The truth of histories may be examined by humanistic disciplines which are different from those that have thus far been considered, disciplines that are necessary for adequate interpretations of historical writings.

II

Questions about the truth of histories are fundamentally of two sorts: (1) How reliable are the historian's facts? (2) How reliable are the conclusions he infers from these facts? In general, these two questions parallel our earlier division between the materials and the principles of relationship in histories. The two questions could be put in other words: (1) What is the evidence for the facts which are the historian's materials? (2) Upon what grounds does the historian conclude that the facts are interrelated as he says they are. The two questions are complexly interwoven, because it is not always possible to make a truly sharp distinction between fact and inference. But we may attempt to think of them separately by considering, for example, Gibbon's statement: "The

Praetorian bands, whose licentious fury was the first symptom and cause of the decline of the Roman empire, scarcely amounted to the last-mentioned number."[15] Here we may ask questions which appear to be factual: Were the Praetorian guards as few in number as Gibbon indicates? Were they characterized by licentious fury? These two questions are not factual in quite the same sense, but another question is much more inferential in character: Was the fury of these bands "the first symptom and cause of the decline"? The number of the guards could be counted and their behavior observed. Whether their behavior was a cause of the decline cannot be simply observed; the writer must relate the facts in this statement to other facts before he can draw such a conclusion.

In the remainder of this chapter we shall consider questions about historical evidence and historical inference. Concerning evidence we shall first inquire into the sources of evidence, and next into the ways in which historians (or readers) may test their evidence.

Evidence

The sources of historical evidence. The sources of a historian's evidence depend, of course, upon the kind of history he is writing, and this whole topic is therefore subject to qualifications which have already been made in our discussion of the subject matter and aims of historians.

Traces of the past are the fundamental form of evidence, for traces include not only physical remains, like ruins and monuments, but what is basic to all history, memory; even verbal accounts of the past are themselves traces. Nevertheless, we may roughly divide historical evidence into two kinds: accounts of the past, and traces of the past.

The historian may himself be an eyewitness to history and may thus find the evidence for what he writes in his own memory. One very bulky category of historical writings, memoirs, is built largely upon the memory of the writer. Thucydides tells us that he him-

---

[15] *Decline and Fall*, p. 91.

self heard some of the speeches he records, and there are many other events in his history which he could have witnessed. Leon Trotsky, in his *History of the Russian Revolution,* also writes about things he witnessed, although he explicitly disapproves of the historian's relying upon his memory.

If we think of a trace as a footprint we may see what is chiefly meant by traces, as opposed to accounts. The footprint of a man is evidence of the presence of a man, even if this presence has been forgotten by the man himself and was witnessed by no other man. This is an example of only one kind of trace, and we shall treat traces in more detail later on. We shall first consider accounts of the past, for this is what we do in everyday life. When we wish to find out about something, we usually try to get the story from someone else who knows about it. The historian as well as the ordinary man relies heavily on verbal accounts; the accounts he turns to may rely on other accounts, so that the verbal chain is sometimes very long.

The accounts of the past which the historian may use as evidence are of two sorts, oral and written. In general, ancient writers made more use of oral accounts than modern writers do. An oral account may come to a historian from an eyewitness or only after it has been handed down through many generations. It is often hard to tell, from a passage itself, how long the oral chain was. Consider the words "they say," "the Persian story," and "according to their authors," in the first paragraphs of Herodotus' history. There are no dates given, and it is not possible to tell, from this paragraph alone, how old the account was, or even whether it was oral or written. In the succeeding paragraphs it becomes clear that the account was very ancient indeed, but Herodotus never tells us very precisely who it was who told him this story.

Modern historians may use oral testimony if they are writing about something in the not too distant past, but they seldom depend on long oral traditions, unless nothing more reliable is available. The written word, for all its ambiguities, is the best way of fixing accounts of the past, that is, of minimizing the ways in which accounts can vary as they are handed down through many generations. This is one reason why written records constitute the greatest single source of historical evidence today. Also, if an oral tradition is once broken it is lost forever, whereas a writing may be unread for centuries and still serve as evidence for a historian who calls new attention to it.

Let us turn now to traces. These include all the facts which a historian may use as evidence but which were not deliberately left by men as historical accounts. Sticking to human rather than natural history, we may still refer to a large body of physical facts which testify to the past existence of various kinds of human activity. Prehistoric wall paintings, ruins of ancient buildings, ancient tools, weapons, coins, and other artifacts can serve as evidence. Political constitutions and laws are not written for the purpose of recording what has happened; but they bear witness to activities and attitudes of men of the past. The whole body of humanistic products is a very valuable source of evidence. This sort of evidence may include poetry and other forms of fine art, as well as histories, written by other historians. These histories do not provide the same kind of evidence as that found in the written records mentioned in the preceding paragraph. For even if the historian has reason to disbelieve a written history and therefore does not use it as a source of information about that history's subject, it is still a historical fact that the earlier historian said what he did, and this may give us important information about his own times and circumstances. It may be false history that Russians invented the telephone and the airplane; it may be true history that Russian historians at one time said that Russians invented the telephone and the airplane. It is similar with other forms of literature. The dramatist may or may not have had historical aims; but in either case his plays may be important sources of information about events or institutions of bygone times; at the very least they constitute a source of information about the dramatist, and to know about him is to know something about the culture in which he appeared.

There are some products of past cultures which most men seldom think of as products of the past, simply because they are so much a part of present culture. These are such things as customs, institutions, and language. The historian may make inferences from these; that is, he may use them as evidence about the past. For example, certain characteristics of the English language can be traced to Anglo-Saxon origins and may provide evidence about Anglo-Saxon customs or living conditions. Similarly, modern legal and political institutions can be traced to ancient origins and may serve as part of the evidence which the historian uses in reconstructing the past.

This brief summary is enough to suggest ways of recognizing the kinds of evidence which historians use. The kind of evidence a historian chooses will depend on what he is able to find, and on his ideas about the best form of evidence. Any evidence may be fallible, and a good historian will employ certain tests to make sure his evidence is as accurate as possible.

Tests of the validity of historical evidence. We can see the nature of the problem of testing evidence if we imagine an instance where we have two contradictory reports about the same thing. We may notice, first, that the presence of the two reports makes us hesitate to accept either one without careful examination. The absence, then, of contradictory evidence tends to make any given piece of evidence credible; so an early step in testing evidence is to look for contradictory evidence.

Once we recognize that it is necessary to examine the evidence, there are two points of view from which we may start. We may ask, first, which reporter is most credible. Second, we may ask which report is most credible; that is, which is more probable, which has more internal consistency, and which harmonizes more fully with other known facts. The student's task here is a double one. He should notice how far a historian applies tests like those discussed below; he should also learn to apply these tests himself to the histories he reads. His attention should be primarily on the former; for, one of the best ways to learn to be critical of historical writings is to understand the critical techniques of reputable historians.

Tests of the first sort ask whether the reporter was able and willing to tell the truth. When the author explicitly says what his source is, he is offering the reader some sort of warrant for what he writes. He may or may not explicitly comment on the source's ability or willingness to tell the truth; but he gives the reader some basis for raising these questions himself. We have already noticed how Herodotus begins by saying he got his story from the Persians. He does not say which Persians, but he does say that they were "the best informed in history." Our willingness to accept Herodotus' estimate of the credibility of his sources will depend on the extent to which Herodotus himself wins our confidence. A little later he says, "The Phoenicians, however, as regards Io, vary from the Persian statements." He withholds comment upon this variation, and goes on to "point out the person who first within my knowledge inflicted injury on the Greeks." The person he points out is Croesus, and since Croesus lived almost one hundred years before Herodotus, "my own knowledge" does not mean what we might think it to mean. For much of the story of Croesus Herodotus does not cite his evidence. He does say that he received information from those in charge of the oracle at Delphi, but it is not easy to tell how much he got from them, and how much from unspecified sources. It is not strange that Delphi should have been a fruitful source of historical information, since kings often sought advice there, and in order to get it they had to be rather explicit about the problems they were facing. Also, they paid for this advice with costly gifts, and those gifts—still presumably visible in Herodotus' time—were good evidence of the wealth and power of the kings who gave them; Herodotus refers several times to gifts which he saw there. Notice that these gifts are traces of the past. In general, traces are perhaps more important as tests or confirmations of evidence than as major sources of evidence.

Thucydides, in this respect, is not unlike the recent historian Leon Trotsky. In the main body of their writings neither tells the reader very much about particular sources of particular pieces of evidence; but, in their introductory pages, each tries to assure the reader that the greatest care has been used in testing evidence. In Thucydides we read:

43

And with reference to the narrative of events, far from permitting myself to derive it from the first source that came to hand, I did not even trust my own impressions, but it rests partly on what I saw myself, partly on what others saw for me, and accuracy of the report being always tried by the most severe and detailed tests possible. My conclusions have cost me some labour from the want of coincidence between accounts of the same occurrences by different eye-witnesses, arising sometimes from imperfect memory, sometimes from undue partiality for one side or the other.[16]

Notice that Thucydides explains imperfections by referring, first, to the inability of eyewitnesses to report the truth ("imperfect memory") and, second, to unwillingness ("undue partiality"). Trotsky writes, in the Preface to his *History of the Russian Revolution:*

This work will not rely in any degree upon personal recollections. The circumstance that the author was a participant in the events does not free him from the obligation to base his exposition upon strictly verified documents. . . .

The sources of this book are innumerable periodical publications, newspapers and journals, memoirs, reports, and material, partly in manuscript, but the greater part published by the Institute of the History of the Revolution in Moscow and Leningrad. We have considered it superfluous to make reference in the text to particular publications, since that would only bother the reader.[17]

Trotsky's attitude is not characteristic of modern scholarly historians. It is now common practice to make frequent reference to sources in footnotes. Gibbon, although he is not exactly modern, exemplifies this procedure. On almost every page of his *Decline and Fall* we find footnote references to books which Gibbon used as sources. The sheer quantity and variety of Gibbon's sources testifies to his great diligence and care in testing many accounts against one another. He is sometimes content merely to cite a

---

[16] *Complete Writings*, p. 14.

[17] Leon Trotsky, *The History of the Russian Revolution*, trans. Max Eastman (Ann Arbor: University of Michigan Press, 1932), pp. xx, xxii.

source, and sometimes he criticizes it, either directly or obliquely. His first footnote reads as follows:

[1] Dion Cassius (l. liv. [c. 8] p. 736) with the annotations of Reimer, who has collected all that Roman vanity has left upon the subject.

Gibbon, referring to the defeat of the Roman general Crassus by the Parthians, hints broadly that the Roman historians are not altogether willing to treat this battle in complete detail, since it reflected little credit upon Roman arms.

Liberal use of footnote citations does not mean that the author expects the reader to test his book by looking up all the sources. Being given the opportunity to check up on what is said strengthens the reader's confidence in what he reads, even if he does not often avail himself of this opportunity. And if the reader is a learned man (Gibbon rather expected his readers to be learned), he will already have some idea about the reliability of the source referred to; even if he is not very learned, he can easily determine the general reputation of the sources. (We should not conclude that writers use footnote citations only in order to make their books more credible. Many of the notes say, as it were: "If you wish to find out more about this matter, see so-and-so.")

If the author does cite his source, he may or he may not explicitly criticize it. But the critical reader will ask whether the source is able and willing to give correct information. These questions are like the questions asked about a witness in a law court. Is the witness *able* to give an accurate report? Was he there? Is he intelligent enough to understand what he saw? Was he sufficiently stable emotionally to see clearly? What is his reputation for accuracy of observation? Is the witness *willing* to give an accurate report? What is his reputation for honesty? What prejudices is he likely to have? In general we suspect testimony when it favors the side toward which the witness is prejudiced. Conversely, we tend to think testimony is true if it favors the side which the witness dislikes. But it is often difficult to discover a historian's prejudices.

Tests of the second sort ask how well the account fits our general experience. Experience leads us to expect consistency in things; we expect them to be consistent with themselves and with other aspects of our experience. We therefore tend to be skeptical of accounts which contain contradictions, or which do not harmonize with our general experience, even if these accounts come to us from apparently trustworthy witnesses.

This is not merely a negative matter. Not only does inconsistency shake our confidence in a book; a high degree of internal consistency does much to win our confidence, apart from all other tests of validity. If an account is not only consistent but also contains a great many circumstantial details, it seems even more reliable. We probably feel, in such cases, that it is simpler to assume the story's truth than to assume it could have been invented, since it would be very difficult to invent so complicated a story and to make it self-consistent. An intricate story is difficult to fabricate, and we should not expect a writer to go to all this trouble without a good reason; so if we suspect that the story is fabricated, we should seek a motive for the fabrication. We should not forget, however, that expert liars are aware of all this, and are skillful in constructing highly circumstantial and yet consistent fictions. The historian need not be deliberately deceitful; it might be merely that his desire to harmonize a vast quantity of circumstantial details has misled him into constructing an overingenious intellectual pattern.

Stories of miracles are extreme examples of accounts which do not agree with our general experience, and many of these are internally consistent and guaranteed by reputable witnesses. We still hesitate to believe them, because they go against other aspects of our experience and make it impossible for us to have a consistent view of our world. When people do accept miracles, they usually appeal to supernatural agencies and thus try to fit the miracles into their experience by widening their frame of reference beyond strictly natural bounds.

We should not insist that historical accounts must correspond

46

exactly to our previous knowledge. We tend to accept an account if it exemplifies a further development of what we already know. Suppose, for example, that a historian relates an event which seems incredible, because it is something that does not happen in our own day. Let us say that the event is a human religious sacrifice. We can believe this because we know that attitudes toward religion undergo great changes and that these changes have profound effects upon behavior, even in our own culture.

Sometimes evidence is confirmed by appealing to some special form of knowledge, rather than to general experience. This is clear in certain forms of "natural" history, like geology, where strictly geological evidence is confirmed by the presence of fossils which may be interpreted in the light of scientific knowledge about biology. Evidence for human history can also be confirmed by appeals to fields of knowledge such as psychology, sociology, or politics. Accounts of the behavior of men or groups can be confirmed if psychology or sociology tell us that men or groups of men behave in a certain way in certain circumstances. Since so much written history is political in character, the historian often selects as evidence the sort of thing which is confirmed by the political theories he holds. This is why we often think we can reconstruct a writer's political beliefs if we understand his historical writings.

We have surveyed the kinds of evidence which historians may employ, and the manners in which they and their readers may test the validity of that evidence. We shall turn finally to ways in which readers can determine the validity of the structures which historians build out of such evidence.

The Validity of Historical Inferences

Writers build historical constructions by connecting facts with one another. The connections we must examine now are the connections which historians establish by making inferences.

In general, it is the task of logic to find appropriate tests for inferences. But even common sense is critical of inferences, and the general reader of history should learn to be critical of the sorts of inference which commonly lead from historical subject matter to historical conclusions.

Historians often make generalizations on the basis of a limited number of particular facts. For example, a historian might analyze the records of shoemakers' guilds in fourteenth-century Germany and conclude: "The medieval guilds were primarily concerned with maintaining high prices for their products through controlling production and the number of producers as well as through direct price regulation." The validity of this generalization can be tested by raising a number of questions. What bases are there for believing (1) that what was true of shoemakers' guilds was true of guilds generally, (2) that what was true of the fourteenth century was true of the Middle Ages generally, (3) that what was true of German guilds was true of guilds generally, and so on? Even if we could find satisfactory bases for all these inferences we could ask whether the historian had made a fair sampling of the records of fourteenth-century shoemakers' guilds in Germany; if he had not, his simplest generalization could not stand. If such generalizations are solidly based, they can of course be combined with other valid generalizations, and conclusions of much higher generality may legitimately be inferred. There is no reason, in principle, why historical generalizations cannot be made the basis of generalizations about the basic nature of all economic associations.

Other historical inferences involve some notion of causation. We may infer from a given fact that certain other facts must have preceded it or followed it. Nothing can occur unless its necessary conditions are fulfilled; if events occur, we can infer that their necessary conditions must have occurred. If we find a brick house we know that a man who knew how to lay bricks must have been in this place. There are things which are generally followed by other things. We can infer, from the occurrence of one of the first things, that one of the other things probably occurred also. If we know that a man fell overboard in mid-ocean, we may be pretty certain that he drowned. Tests for both types of inferences are fairly obvious. When a historian infers the existence of a necessary condition of some established fact, he must be sure about two things: (1) that the fact is really established, and (2) that there is only one way it could have come about. Suppose a stone tablet 2,500 years old, engraved with Greek words, is found on a certain island. The historian could infer that Greek-speaking people were on this island 2,500 years ago, but only under certain conditions. He would have to know that the tablet was 2,500 years old, and that the words were Greek; he would also have to be sure that the tablet was not carried to the island long after it was engraved, or that it was not engraved by non-Greek people who knew the Greek language, and sometimes wrote in Greek for special reasons. When inferring the probable consequences of a known fact, the historian must again be sure that the basic fact is really known. Did the man really fall overboard? If he did, how certain can we be of the consequences? Was there no chance that he might have been saved?

Of these two types, we can never be as certain about inferences to probable consequences as we can sometimes be about inferences to necessary conditions. Probable consequences can be prevented; but children never occur without parents, artifacts are made only by human beings, and great books can only be written by wise men. If we see a man killed by a gunshot, we know that the gun must have been loaded; if we know that a gun is loaded, we cannot be sure it will kill. If we know that a man is wise, we still cannot be sure he will write a book; but if we know there is wisdom in a book, we can be sure its author was wise.

By combining a number of established facts, inferences to necessary conditions or probable consequences can, of course, be greatly strengthened; but this procedure would introduce no essentially new modes of inference. Different sets of records can testify to the presence of a given man in a given place at a given time. Any one of these records might be in error, but the different records support one another, if they are really different. If nine different records are all based upon a tenth, they are all subject to any errors which may be embodied in the tenth, and the ten sets of records are not really different. But if a man's name is found on a certain hotel register of a certain date, and if the police of the same town report his arrest for speeding on that same date, and if the local newspapers report that he delivered a public speech there at that time, we may be fairly certain that he was in this town at that time. It is not likely that all three records could be wrong.

The validity of any case of inference involving causation depends on the validity of the writer's beliefs or theories about the relations between antecedents and consequences. Ultimately, questions about such beliefs or theories can lead to very difficult philosophical problems. We can never be more certain about the validity of any historical account than we are about the resolution of the philosophical problems concerning sequences of events. The mere fact that one event follows another never convinces us that the first is the necessary condition of the second, or that the second is the consequence of the first. When historians claim that there really were connections like these, they must have some belief or theory about causation. The careful reader can determine what these beliefs or theories are and can test them against his own most careful reflections about these problems. He must, of course, reach a very high level of critical ability before he can judge, with confidence, the theories which guide the mature historian in his work.

Chapter 3

Drama and Fiction

Many of the problems involved in the reading of dramatic literature are like problems involved in the reading of narrative literature. The remarks on drama in the first part of this chapter are therefore intended to apply, with some modification, to narratives too. The last part considers problems that are more or less special to the reading either of dramatic literature, or of narrative literature.[1]

The attitude the reader should have if he is properly to understand a novel or play is not the same as the attitude he should have in reading a history. Consider the distinction made above in the chapter on history between the past and statements about the past. Is there an analogous distinction in drama and fiction? This is a question of a distinction between statements, and what the statements refer to. Common sense seems to say that the statements of fiction do not refer to something outside themselves, in the sense in which historical statements do. To be sure, history can be dramatically presented, and some novels are called historical novels; some histories read like novels, and some novels and plays read like histories, and are even called histories. But the reader's attitude toward fiction, even when it seems most like history, is not the same as his attitude toward strictly historical writing.

The statements of fiction do, of course, refer to something. But in fiction, more than in history, the reader expects the statements

---

[1] This chapter is intended to be read along with a careful study of Shakespeare's *Macbeth*. The questions raised are meant, however, not as a guide to the reader's interpretation of *Macbeth*, but as suggestions of procedures he may profitably follow in his study of plays and novels generally.

themselves to determine the character of the things they refer to, as well as the relations among these things. The statements of a novel, like a painting, may construct the idea of a person, a character; and the reader would not need to think (any more than the observer of the painting would) that the artist wishes him to believe that the represented character precisely corresponds, either as a whole character, or in certain particular features, to some individual person who has actually lived, or to particular characteristics that have actually been embodied in one person or another. Rather, the character is held up, so to speak, before the reader's mind for him to experience as a possible existence. Further, the portrayed character may be involved, in the novel, in sequences of action; the reader does not take the author to mean that these sequences ever actually occurred, or even that they are necessarily like sequences that actually occur. On the contrary, writers of fiction often deliberately represent sequences of events significantly different from those our experience would lead us to accept. Here too the reader permits the statements of the book to determine the character of these sequences of events.

Credibility in fiction is significantly different from credibility in history. In history, the reader expects the sequences of events to correspond to sequences that have actually occurred; he tends to disbelieve, and therefore to condemn as history, statements which represent sequences which general experience leads him to think unlikely or impossible. The expectations of the reader of fiction are controlled to a much greater extent by all the statements within the book itself. He "believes in" the actions of a given character if they are "in character," that character having been created to a large extent by the statements in the book. He finds a sequence of events "credible" because they are consistent with other parts of the book, even if not with the world of ordinary experience.

The reading of history, more than the reading of fiction, leads the reader to consider whether the statements he reads correspond to his experience of the world outside the book. He will therefore have to limit, more than the reader of fiction will, the amount of attention he can devote to considering the internal relationships

that hold the various parts of the book together. Historical literature, like fiction, can be well organized, but the discipline of reading fiction is concerned in a special way with finding the internal
structures of the writings it studies.

Because of the importance of the question of truth, in the reading of history, two objects of study were distinguished in the chapter on history: understanding what the history says, and determining whether this is true. A similar distinction is not very rewarding
in the reading of drama and fiction. In them, however, there is a
factor that is much more important than it is in history, and that
is the emotions or feelings of the reader. As he reads drama and
fiction he should reflect on his feelings, not only because they are
so important an element of the reading experience, but also because
they provide good ways of testing his grasp of the work's structure. If the structure as he grasps it does not adequately conform
to the emotions he actually feels, then there is likely to be something wrong with his grasp. In the following pages our reflections
will have primary reference to the structure of the work and to the
feelings of the reader.

I

The series of questions now proposed about Shakespeare's *Macbeth* are intended to suggest procedures which can help the reader
move toward an adequate interpretation of any play or novel.
The order in which questions are proposed is unimportant. Different points of departure, and different sequences of questions,
may be appropriate for different works, different readers, and
different discussion groups. The procedures described, and the
various progressions from one question to another, are to be
understood as procedures of a sort that might take place, not
procedures that should be rigidly limited. But the reader should
not be satisfied with his interpretation of a work until he has considered, in some order or other, a full range of approaches comparable to that suggested below.

The proposed questions are of two complementary sorts: (1)
questions of interpretation, by means of which the reader should

try to formulate his understanding of the play as a whole; (2) questions of analysis, by means of which he should try to break the play down into significant parts, of one sort or another. These two kinds of questions are closely related. The answer to a question of one kind can serve as the occasion for raising a new question of the other kind, in a process which is not expected to lead to a final interpretation; this chapter assumes that great literature is not easily exhausted, even by the questions that intelligent readers may raise over a period of centuries. Nevertheless, the reader should take as his main aim the formulation of an interpretation that will account, with some adequacy, for the effect of the work as a whole, and for the functions and interrelationships of its parts. But he should pursue this aim patiently. Understanding of profound works is the result of a ripening process which may take a very long time—scholars profitably spend lifetimes in the study of great literature.

The author of a play intends its effect to be produced by its comparatively uninterrupted performance upon the stage. The reflective reader should never forget this, for many reflective procedures are not strictly compatible with this mode of "reading" a play. No matter how detailed his reflections become, the reader should place their results in their proper context: a whole play intended to be comprehended within the space (ordinarily) of not much more than two or three hours. He should begin his study of a play like *Macbeth* by seeing a performance of the play. This is of course not always feasible; if it is not, the first acquaintance with the play should be as much like seeing it as possible.[2] Nowadays performances of plays are often recorded, but the student should be careful in using recordings, since they so often drastically cut the play; the reader should follow the text while listening to a recording. It may be that several persons can read the play together,

---

[2] This suggestion can, with qualifications, be adapted to the reading of novels. The initial reading of fiction should be comparatively rapid and unreflective; the reader should try first to see the book as a whole. Full-size novels do, however, present special difficulties because of their length and can hardly be read as rapidly as most plays; and reflection can less easily be postponed to a second or third reading.

aloud. At the very least the solitary reader can read the play completely through with no more interruption than he would experience if he went to the theater. It should be noted, however, that there are serious limitations to these approximations to theatrical presentation. The way in which one reads a scene, a speech, a line, or a word, can depend a great deal upon one's interpretation of the whole play, or at least of large parts of the play. The reader would have to be clairvoyant to know what words to emphasize at the beginning of a play, if he does not yet know what this beginning is leading up to; this is particularly true of the dramatic forms of literature which make great capital out of such elements as suspense and surprise. But there is a corresponding disadvantage to seeing a theatrical performance: every detail in such a performance, particularly if it is an intelligent one, is controlled by an already formed interpretation. This could be a handicap to a reader in that it interferes with his working out his own interpretation.

When the reader has completed his first rapid reading of *Macbeth*, and before he goes on to more reflective reading, he should formulate a statement (and he should actually write it out) which summarizes as briefly as possible his understanding of the play at this time. He might write:

> Macbeth, a nobleman and warrior with a reputation for loyalty and bravery, becomes ambitious to rule Scotland. He acquires the throne by murdering Duncan, the king, and exiles Duncan's sons. Some of the nobles become suspicious; Macbeth fears their suspicions and commits atrocities against them in an effort to strengthen his hold upon the throne. These tyrannical acts drive the nobles into open rebellion, in the course of which Macbeth is defeated in battle and killed by Macduff; Duncan's son Malcolm is placed on the throne.[3]

Such a statement would not be likely to satisfy most persons who have seen the play and have been strongly moved by it. This does not matter for our purposes. It gives us a starting point. It is not

---

[3] The summary might, of course, follow quite different lines, if the reader thought something other than action was of central importance in the play.

enough merely to express dissatisfaction with this synopsis; the reflective reader needs to know why it is unsatisfactory. He may seek the reason by considering whether or not the statement adequately accounts for certain details he may remember from the play (which does not necessarily mean that these details ought to be expressly mentioned in the interpretation).

The search for details with which to test and to develop an interpretation (any statement that attempts to summarize the reader's understanding of the whole play is here called an interpretation) should not be haphazard, but systematic. Traditional modes of analyzing a play (i.e., breaking it up into its parts) will be useful. One traditional mode goes back to Aristotle, who, in his *Poetics*, suggested analyzing a play in terms of plot, character, thought, diction, melody, and spectacle. Analysis can be carried on in such terms without committing oneself to an Aristotelian point of view; and it can help keep an analysis from becoming haphazard. One need not necessarily begin with plot or with character or with any other of these elements. Much depends upon the play, and the reader can rely on his own feelings as a guide to what is of special importance in the play, at least in getting his analysis under way. Generally speaking, most readers with most good plays tend to be particularly struck, at first, by certain incidents (and these are parts of the plot), or by certain characters. Some spectators or readers may be especially struck by something like the soliloquies in *Hamlet;* and what interests them here may come under the heading of thought or diction, rather than of plot or character; or, in *Macbeth*, if the scenes with the witches seem especially striking, the reader's attention could be said to be focused on the element of spectacle.

Let us say that the reader of *Macbeth* begins to develop his analysis by considering the characters in the play. One advantage in such a beginning is that it is easy to refresh one's memory on this point by looking over the list of *dramatis personae*. The reader might ask himself, "Does my summary slight or exaggerate the importance of any of the characters?" In the statement given above, only Macbeth, Duncan, Macduff, and Malcolm are mentioned by name. It is hardly possible to establish a definitive hierarchy of characters in the order of their dramatic importance, but it is useful to consider them in this way. The dramatic importance of a character depends upon his relationship to other characters, and to the events that take place in the play. A king, like Duncan, may not have the same importance in the play that he presumably has in the society the play represents. It is more than likely that if Macbeth is the hero of the play his wife will have great dramatic importance, even though her social status is lower than that of Malcolm, a comparatively unimportant character.

Simple relationships, such as husband and wife, father and son, ruler and subject, master and servant, are important; the reader must be clear about them. Other sorts of relationship must also be considered. How, for example, are the characters related to one another in terms of interests, attitudes, or purposes? Some provisional answers to such questions might be the following: Lady Macbeth and Macbeth share a common purpose. Macbeth and Macduff have conflicting purposes. But these answers need qualifications. Lady Macbeth and Macbeth differ markedly in their attitudes toward what is involved in the attainment of their common objective, so much so that there could be said to be a real conflict between them. And Macbeth and Macduff, for all their antagonism, have similar attitudes toward military bravery, and it could even be argued that Macbeth's attitude toward his own crimes resembles Macduff's attitude more than Lady Macbeth's. The importance of such considerations can be tested by the reader's feelings about them. Is the total effect of the play strongly colored by the complex relationship between Macbeth and his wife? The reader probably feels that it is, even before he understands the play well enough to explain why it is.

Lines of inquiry like this can be carried far, but just how far they should be carried cannot be determined in the early stages of analysis. Certainly there will be many temptations to shift the analysis toward other terms. The importance of the relationship between Macbeth and Macduff, for example, is in large part the result of the slaughter of Macduff's family. This, being an event, might lead the analysis into questions about the interconnections of various events, for example, into a discussion of plot or action. In general it is good for a reader, or for a discussion group, to undergo the discipline of holding for a while to one idea, such as character. Reflection should continue along the chosen line as long as it seems sufficiently fruitful. As other questions naturally arise, however, the reader (or member of a discussion group) would do well to jot them down in a notebook for reference at a later stage of analysis. When good occasion seems to arise for shifting the terms of analysis the reader should attempt once again to formulate an interpretation of the play as a whole. This new formulation is sure to differ in important respects from the earlier one. It is important for the reader to notice how his interpretation develops as his analysis becomes more detailed and thorough, and to get continual practice in formulating interpretative statements. Even if no good occasion offers itself for shifting the analysis from terms, say, of character to those of action, the reader should periodically interrupt his analytic procedures and take his bearings, by making new efforts to formulate an interpretation of the play as a whole.

A reader who has proceeded in the suggested manner might, as a result of his reflections, be dissatisfied with his original statement for a number of reasons. It might now seem to him that the role of Lady Macbeth should be brought out, and that the nature of the struggle in which Macbeth is involved should be more closely related to the thoughts he expressed in his arguments with her and in his famous soliloquies. For the statement as it stands suggests too much that the conflict is a material and physical struggle between Macbeth and his external enemies; the reader's analysis is likely to suggest that the conflict is really spiritual and moral and that it involves not merely Macbeth and his enemies but the one person nearest to him (his wife) and the conflicting elements within his own soul. The essential features of the struggle may now seem narrower in scope than any struggle involving many persons. On the other hand, the struggle may appear to transcend the narrow bounds of a few persons, or even of the nation, since the forces in it are of perennial importance to all men and suggest problems that could be called universal and eternal. Suppose the reader now interprets the play in this way:

> Macbeth, who has earned distinction in an honorable life, is acutely sensitive to the struggle of good and evil forces in the world. He is susceptible to the appeal of the evil forces, and this susceptibility is cultivated by his wife, who drives him toward evil, even though his sensitivity to goodness makes him reluctant to follow her directions. As he proceeds in his evil career the struggle between good and evil locates itself more definitely within Macbeth's own heart, and again evil wins out. But Macbeth never loses his sensitivity to goodness, and therefore becomes an evildoer who suffers extremely through his awareness of the good he is losing in his pursuit of evil (because of his realization of the moral significance of his actions). Even in his final destruction he displays something of virtue, i.e., courage, but his very virtues are tarnished with the consequences of his evil-doing, which has reduced him to desperation, a situation in which his courage is more that of a cornered animal, than of a man.

Now a reader whose reflections had gone no further than those that have been suggested would not be likely to formulate a statement like this one. It has been deliverately contrived to make a sharp contrast with the original statement. The interpretation we started with might be called materialistic, concerned with very concrete particulars; the new interpretation might be called spiritual or moral and is more abstract in its references. A reader who presented such a "spiritual" interpretation to a discussion group might be asked to defend it by showing how it accounts for certain concrete details, such as the appearances of the weird sisters. He could answer that what is referred to as Macbeth's acute sensitivity to the forces of good and evil, and his susceptibility to the temptations of the latter, are shown in the scene where he is confronted by the weird sisters, and that Banquo's presence in this scene and his reactions to what he hears show that it is not only Macbeth who is exposed to these forces and that there is more than one possible reaction to them. Many other concrete details could be accounted for in a similar manner.

Testing an interpretation by reference to particular details of the play returns the reader to analysis. It will often be useful to test the interpretation by reference to details brought out by analysis along lines that have been ignored—in this case, by reference to details of the action. (This is not, however, to deny that it could also be useful to return to terms that have governed earlier stages of analysis.) A start can be made by asking oneself whether there is any striking detail that has thus far seemed unduly neglected. The reader might consider, for example, the scene in which Lady Macbeth walks in her sleep and tries to wash imaginary blood from her hands. This scene hardly seems to be accounted for by either of the two interpretations, and it provokes a host of questions. What has happened to the relationship between Macbeth and his wife? Earlier in the play they are represented as very close to each other, and now, in this scene, they have come to inhabit different worlds, and each of them is utterly alone. How does it happen that Lady Macbeth, who seemed to be the stronger of the two characters in the first part of the play, later seems the weaker? She breaks completely under the terrible strain brought on by her memories of what has long since passed. Macbeth, whatever else one may say about him, has weathered the terrible strain of the past and is facing new troubles, not retreating from them. Attempts to answer such questions should rest upon disciplined analysis. Therefore the reader should consider the scene systematically, in its relationships with other preceding and succeeding events. From what other events does this occurrence follow? To what other events does it lead? And questions of this sort should be controlled by an effort to find one central line of action to which all events are related in some specifiable way.

The answers to such questions will depend very much upon the terms one uses in interpreting the central action of the play: whether one uses terms of physical and mental action, as in the first interpretation, or terms of spiritual and moral values, as in the second. One cannot know in advance which sort of interpretation will work out best. A continual process of testing proposed interpretations against different analytic procedures should bring the reader closer and closer to an adequate understanding of the work.

Making a fresh start, the reader may proceed to relate the sleep-walking scene, as an event, to other important actions. He may begin by asking how it is connected with the rise and fall of Macbeth's external fortunes. There are, indeed, many aspects of the scene which could steer us away from the question of external fortunes. In itself, the scene is primarily concerned with showing us something internal, the inside of Lady Macbeth's mind, rather than anything external. It is not caused by the events that have most directly brought about the present precarious state of Macbeth's external affairs; nor does it cause this state of affairs. Still, there are reasons for keeping our attention focused upon external (material and physical) things. Their tangibility affords a good foothold. Even if the main significance of the scene can be accounted for in internal terms, the internal (the things of the spirit) is always re-lated to the external in human life. And it must be of special sig-nificance that the scene occurs in a context where Macbeth (and the reader too, no doubt) is very much preoccupied with his ex-ternal fortunes. Even if the result of this inquiry into the intercon-nections of external events turns out to be negative and sheds little direct light upon the dramatic significance of the sleepwalking scene, it is sure to illuminate other features of the play.

The proposed inquiry is concerned with tying the major events of the play together and then fitting the sleepwalking scene into the pattern. The events can be tied together in a way suggested by the analogy of a great river system, in which a main stream follows a course affected at various points by the confluence of tributary streams. Thus, for example, we could trace the biography of a man up to the year 1900, when he became involved with a man who greatly influenced his future career. We might wish, then, to trace the biography of this second man before 1900, in order better to understand why he influenced our main subject's career as he did. Any number of other men might come within the scope of our inquiry, but the first man would remain our main subject: his ca-reer would be the main stream, and the careers of the other men the tributaries. Suppose this were tried with the story of Macbeth, with the ultimate intention of seeing how Lady Macbeth's sleep-walking is related to that part of Macbeth's career with which the play is chiefly concerned.

A sketch of the main line of Macbeth's story could begin as follows. His encounter with the weird sisters suggests to him an exciting possibility, the acquisition of the throne, and he tells his wife about this. She conceives a plan for bringing this future possibility into reality and conspires with him to murder Duncan. The plot against Duncan is successful and Macbeth becomes king. It is easy to see how this sketch of the main action could be completed. Other lines of action, like tributary streams, are the stories of Banquo and Macduff. Banquo was present at the original encounter with the weird sisters, and the sisters' references to him cause anxiety in Macbeth, an anxiety which leads him ultimately to murder Banquo and to attempt to murder Banquo's son, Fleance; and their references to Macduff, along with other portents, lead him to slaughter Macduff's family when Macduff himself escapes from his power. The stories of Macduff and his family bear upon the rebellion which finally brings about the collapse of Macbeth's external fortunes.[4]

---

[4] These lines of action are not typical of subsidiary actions in tragedies, because they undergo very little actual development within the play. In fact, *Macbeth* is not a good play for illustrating subsidiary lines of a complicated action; this is one reason why it is an unusually short play. Macbeth's career is indeed affected by Banquo's, but not primarily because of what Banquo has been or done. It is in anticipation of Banquo's possible effect upon the future that Macbeth takes action against him; he fears Banquo himself, but, still more, he is troubled by the idea that he has given his own soul to the devil, only to make the seed of Banquo kings in the distant future. This future possibility does bear upon Macbeth's own career, since he takes important action in an effort to prevent what is going to happen; and this action by Macbeth has serious consequences for the main action. We are also told very little about Macduff (the reference to the manner in which he was born is, indeed, a very brief but dramatically important presentation of an event in a subsidiary line), but enough to be able to understand his effect upon the career of Macbeth. In a longer and more complicated action like that of *King Lear*, the subsidiary line of action concerning the fate of Gloucester is presented in great detail in the play.

Now how does the sleepwalking scene fit into this pattern of events? The scene is followed by the death of Lady Macbeth, which contributes to the complete destruction of Macbeth himself; it makes his destruction more complete, but it hardly seems a cause of it. The scene also suggests that Macbeth's downfall should not be understood simply in terms of external fortunes, since the reader will probably regard Lady Macbeth's death as an important part of Macbeth's downfall, but not as a factor in his material downfall.

Perhaps more interesting problems are set by seeking to connect the sleepwalking scene with the events that precede it. The sleepwalking does not seem to be caused by immediately preceding events; rather, it seems to be a consequence of the murder of Duncan, and of the effects of that murder itself (not of its later consequences) upon the mind of Lady Macbeth. Now why does Shakespeare bring this scene in so late in the play, when Macbeth (and the audience too) is preoccupied, not with the murder of Duncan, but with some of its comparatively remote consequences?[5] Is it merely that we need to know what finally happens to Lady Macbeth, lest we ask at the end of the play, "What ever happened to Lady Macbeth?" A simple answer to this question would not help us understand why Lady Macbeth's ultimate fate is presented to the reader when it is. The reader would be satisfied with such an explanation only if he felt that the scene was peripheral or tangential, with no great bearing on what precedes and follows it in Act V, a sort of "By the way, this is what happened to Lady Macbeth."[6]

The difficulty of fitting the sleepwalking scene into the sequence of events immediately preceding it may tempt the reader to con-

---

[5] A question like this is not to be understood as a question about Shakespear's personal reasons for doing what he did.

[6] Sometimes this question ("What ever happened to X?") is just what is needed to clear up a point. Writers are often concerned about mere neatness and like to tidy up their works in this way. It has been remarked that accounting for the fate of each person is a special characteristic of the endings of nineteenth-century novels.

clude that the scene is best treated under the heading of character, rather than action. Does this scene not show us essential differences between the characters of Macbeth and Lady Macbeth? One can hardly deny that it does. And some readers may be satisfied with an explanation along this line. But does it not seem worthwhile anyhow to insist on the question, What is the particular effect of this scene's occurring precisely when it does? This question insists upon considering a sequence of events that take place in time, a consideration likely to be overlooked if we are only comparing characters (unless character development is the issue).

The problem now under consideration provides a good occasion for interrupting the analysis to turn our attention to an approach not yet discussed, even though its basis will surely have had some influence upon any analysis carried thus far. This approach takes its point of departure directly from the reader's feelings. It asks questions of the following sort. How does the reader feel about the various characters involved in any given incident? Where are his sympathies? What is the precise nature of these sympathies? What fears or hopes does he have for the various characters before and after the incidents occur? What does he think about degrees of responsibility for one turn of events or another? Do the characters deserve what happens to them? Or do they deserve better or worse?

Before raising these specific questions about *Macbeth* we should take notice of the fact that it is easier to go wrong with respect to our feelings than it is with respect to the facts. The characters of a play or novel are really there, and so are the incidents; and we can be fairly sure about many of their features, even before we have opportunities to check them against other things. But our sympathies or antipathies are quickly engaged, and if they are misdirected we may take some time to find it out. Ultimately our understanding of a work, which is founded upon analysis, will determine how we feel about the characters and incidents; and if our analysis is thorough, our feelings will be reliable—in fact, it may be impossible to distinguish them from our understanding. But in the early stages of study the reader should be careful about his feelings and realize the necessity of discovering proper foundations for them. With this caution we may proceed to consider how we can reflect upon our feelings as we read, and thus contribute to the development of an interpretation of a play like *Macbeth*.

Let us return to the sleepwalking scene. Do our feelings about it have a bearing upon our feelings about the preceding and following scenes? Just how do we feel about Macbeth at this point in the play? How are our feelings related to hopes or fears we had for him earlier in the play? How do we feel toward Lady Macbeth during this scene? How are these feelings related to earlier feelings about her? And how do all these feelings bear upon our attitude toward Macbeth in the situation in which we find him in Act V?[7]

There are many different orders in which these questions could be considered. Let us begin by assuming that we are, at least to some extent, sorry for Lady Macbeth during the sleepwalking scene. Feelings of pity can be influenced by many considerations. Any human suffering is likely to arouse pity, regardless of its cause or of the capacity of the sufferer to endure or overcome the suffering. If we feel that Lady Macbeth is strong enough to endure her suffering, or is likely to take some action that will relieve her of it, our pity may not be so great. But let us assume that the suffering is

---

[7] The complex interrelations of our dramatic feelings can be illustrated by considering various possible attitudes of a spectator toward another scene, the combat between Macbeth and Macduff. If someone were to enter the theater at the point where the fight begins, he could find his feelings strongly aroused, especially if the actors stage an interesting duel. His feelings might be turned more or less favorably toward Macbeth or Macduff, depending on how much he sees of Act V, scene viii (the last scene in the play), before the start of the duel. Many more considerations enter into the feelings of the alert spectator who has seen and understood the entire play up to this point; he could not simply say, "I am for Macduff and against Macbeth," or vice versa. How distorted a spectator's attitude could be if he were told only, as he entered the theater at the beginning of the duel, that Macduff was trying to avenge Macbeth's murder of Lady Macduff! Or, if he had seen only one earlier scene, the one in which Macduff learns of the slaughter. Our feelings about the death of Macbeth are strongly colored by all the hopes and fears we have had for him throughout the play, and by our sympathy for Macduff, not simply by what Macbeth has done to Macduff.

too much for her to endure, and that she is helpless before it. If this is true it will affect our feelings about her, even if we feel—as we must—that she herself is to a great extent responsible for the situation in which she suffers; feelings about responsibility do affect the degree and quality of our pity. Surely we cannot pity her in the same way we pity a child, like Macduff's little son, the innocent victim of adult brutality.

Suppose we compare our feelings about Macbeth. Do we, in Act V, pity him? If so, hardly in the same way that we pity Lady Macbeth. Does he not seem to have greater powers of endurance? And does he not seem more capable of fighting against the causes of his suffering? If we say yes to these questions, we will see some reason why we have different feelings about Macbeth and Lady Macbeth at this point in the play. The differences themselves are likely to suggest further questions, particularly about the beginning of the play and its bearing on our feelings about Act V.

Our reflections could bring us to say that Macbeth seems, in Act V, to be the stronger and the more active of the two leading characters. Is this to be expected, on the basis of the feelings we had about the two characters in Acts I and II? Hardly. At the beginning Macbeth seemed vacillating, whereas Lady Macbeth had a powerful will which stuck to its purpose and swept everything before it, giving Macbeth strength without which he could not have acted as he did. These differences make us feel differently about the beginning and about the ending of the play. Is it easy to sympathize with Lady Macbeth in the early parts? If Macbeth's strength and cruelty lessen our sympathy for him in Act V, do not Lady Macbeth's strength and cruelty lessen our sympathy for her in Acts I and II? Such reflections might seem to clarify our understanding of the whole play; on the other hand, they might seem to present new difficulties. For, do we not feel that the more a person is responsible for his fate the less we are inclined to pity him when he suffers it? If so, it may seem strange to have more pity for Lady Macbeth than for Macbeth in Act V, if we hold Lady Macbeth chiefly responsible for the murder of Duncan, which was the primary cause of the disasters that finally overcame Macbeth and his wife. Reflections like these are likely to lead the reader to more and more careful analysis of the characters of Macbeth and Lady Macbeth, as they can be seen during the beginning section of the play, and of the extent to which, and the respects in which, their characters are responsible for the events that follow. It is beyond the scope of this chapter to carry any of these lines of questioning very far, but a few suggestions are appropriate.[8]

An analysis of the characters of Macbeth and his wife, particularly as represented in Acts I and II, and an effort to harmonize this analysis with his feelings about the same characters in Act V may lead the reader to conclude that Macbeth must be given the greater share of responsibility for the final catastrophes. It may now appear that Macbeth, throughout the play, understands much better than Lady Macbeth, the full implications of the criminal career they embark upon in Act. I. This can be brought out by comparing their respective attitudes toward the murder of Duncan, before, during, and just after its accomplishment. Are they both apprehensive before the murder? They are. But are their apprehensions of the same sort? Are they equally concerned about the possibility of being found out or punished for the crime? About the immediate and ultimate effects of the crime upon their own souls? About the moral significance of the crime?

After considering questions like these the reader might conclude that Lady Macbeth's psychological breakdown results from her inability to foresee the psychological consequences of her actions, and from her lack of moral fiber, which made her unable to endure the consequences. He might also conclude that Macbeth's early vacillations, and the nature of the shock he manifests at the time of the crime, are due to his full realization of the psychological and moral complexities of the act of murder. And the increasing firmness of his determination to continue in the pursuit of his ambi-

---

[8] The reader should keep in mind that this chapter makes many suggestions which he is by no means expected to accept without question. It is hoped, however, that the scope of the questions, and the understanding they may lead to, illustrate an attempt to improve the reader's ability to give a satisfactory account of every part of the play.

tions, in spite of his knowledge of all these complexities, may be evidence that his will power is very strong indeed—strong enough to help him endure the sufferings that come upon him and fight against the growing power of his enemies. Such reflections may also provoke other questions about the dramatic relationships between Macbeth and his wife. Does she function primarily in order to show, perhaps by contrast, what the true character of Macbeth is? Or to help the reader understand how Macbeth's character changes in the course of the drama? Is her diminishing importance to the action, as the play proceeds, intended to suggest that Macbeth, toward the end of the play, is losing something that he very much needs (as Act I may seem to suggest), or rather that at this point she can no longer help him?[9]

The questions proposed about the chief characters in *Macbeth*, and about the reader's feelings toward these characters, can carry analysis a long way forward. It might well be appropriate, after following such a line of reflection, to attempt once more to formulate a brief interpretation of the whole play. In the light of this further analysis the earlier formulations may seem unsatisfactory. The first formulation, in addition to its neglect of Lady Macbeth, is inadequate in what it says about the feelings and attitudes which complicate Macbeth's actions. It goes too far in suggesting that the central conflict in the play is between Macbeth and the other nobles of scotland. As noted before, the statement puts too much

---

[9] All tragic dramas or novels involve serious conflicts. In some of these the conflicts are between two persons who clearly recognize each other as antagonists. Throughout much of *Hamlet* this is true. In other plays, like *Othello*, the hero does not recognize his antagonist as such. In still other plays, like Sophocles' *Oedipus the King*, the hero can be regarded as his own antagonist, although he wrongly suspects others of antagonistic attitudes. This is to some extent true in *Macbeth*; but one of the peculiarities of *Macbeth* is that the hero has a powerful accomplice in important parts of the play; here the accomplice is also in a sense an antagonist, since she works on only one of the two conflicting sides of Macbeth. Such differences among plays, fascinating in themselves, call attention to considerations which significantly qualify the questions one can raise, and the answers one can propose, about plays and novels.

stress on the physical and material elements and too little on the moral and spiritual, an objection that appears even stronger now. The second interpretation given above is too abstract. It does not specify the nature of Macbeth's inner conflict; nor does it show how and why the conflict is resolved or the various stages of its development. It does, to be sure, suggest a possible reaction, by the reader, to the tragedy of the character of Macbeth, but this re-action is too much like a feeling of satisfaction in the deserved punishment of a wicked criminal; such a feeling would not harmonize with the actual feelings of a perceptive reader. So, let us propose a third interpretation:

Macbeth is a valiant, proud, and ambitious nobleman. The course of events suggests to him, and to his soldier comrade Banquo, possibilities of achieving social and political greatness. Macbeth's powerful imagination makes vivid for him a vast range of implications and consequences, good and evil, of these possibilities. His moral sensitivity restrains him from evil means of achieving greatness, until his wife, who shares his ambitions but is not restrained by imagination or by moral sensitivity, gives him encouragement which proves decisive. They achieve their mutual ambitions by murdering their king, Duncan, but as a consequence each one's peace of mind is shattered. Lady Macbeth, in the concentrated intensity of her original enthusiasm (which she was not able to maintain) had not expected this and does not even struggle to prevent the completion of her destruction. Macbeth had anticipated this loss of peace, before and at the time of the murder, and his desire to regain peace drives him on to commit new crimes, even without Lady Macbeth's support. He has reason to fear Banquo (thinking that he too must be ambitious for greatness) and has him murdered. He has different reasons for fearing Macduff, whose wife and children he murders after Macduff himself escapes his power. These acts do more to ruin than to regain his peace, because a man of Macbeth's imagination and moral sensitivity cannot enjoy peace in the situation resulting from his crimes; and, besides, these atrocities bring about open rebellion on the part of the nobles. The conflict that takes place within Macbeth's soul is reflected and completed in the political conflict represented in the battles and duels of the last act. His moral sensitivity is almost, but not entirely, annihilated by the development his evil potentialities have undergone; the person he has become at the end of the play is destroyed by moral forces represented by the armies led by Malcolm, moral forces he would like to have had on his side. The spectator's feelings are complicated by his understanding of the complexity of Macbeth's character, and by the realization that Macbeth's destruction involves the destruction not only of much that is evil but also of much that is good.

The foregoing suggestions encourage the reader to select the terms of various stages of his analysis in a more or less haphazard way. The progressive development of his interpretation is likely, however, to lead him to attribute special importance to action in one work, to character in another, to thought in yet another, and so on. Analysis along several lines may be useful for any given play or novel, but it is scarcely likely that all such lines will have the same importance in all works. The more thoroughly worked out an interpretation becomes, the more likely it is to make clear that the work being interpreted is primarily concerned with action or character or thought, or some other element. The third interpretation proposed above seems to suggest that *Macbeth* is primarily constructed in terms of a particular development of a particular kind of character; other kinds of interpretation are of course possible for this play; and analysis of a play like *Othello* may more immediately suggest a primary concern for the development of a particular pattern of actions.

Different modes of analysis can be carried on, not in terms of such elements as action, character, and thought, but in terms of sections into which a play or novel can be divided: acts, scenes, speeches, lines, words; or chapters, paragraphs, sentences, and the like. The lines of analysis already discussed are likely to turn in this direction, from time to time, as the present analysis turned to the consideration of a particular scene, the sleepwalking scene. But for many readers it may be well to begin by considering particular sections of the work; or, if a different kind of beginning is made, the reader should not follow it too far before turning, deliberately, to consider the sections, in order to develop a sufficiently comprehensive interpretation.

One of the chief advantages of considering a play or novel in terms of its sections (or of the subdivisions of sections) is that it focuses attention upon the actual order in which the work is presented. A different sort of analysis, in terms of character, for example, may lead the reader to forget that the work has such an order, and that this order is rigid. If one becomes engrossed in the character of Macbeth, forgetting that he manifests traits of his character at different times and in different situations that follow one another in a definite order, one's interpretation may turn out to be of dubious validity.

The reader may begin this mode of analysis by considering one basic fact: any given passage from any novel or play must be thought of as following and preceding other passages in the work (there are two obvious exceptions). The sequences of events represented or narrated in a play or novel are not, however, to be understood as occurring in the same order in which they are presented. This possibility presents interesting questions. The reader should certainly be able to answer two questions: What is the order in which the incidents in the story are understood to occur (the order of occurrence)? What is the order in which the play or novel presents these incidents (the order of presentation)? These two orders are often, perhaps more often than not, different. In general they differ more in novels than in plays, although what we say here depends on how the two orders are defined. How, for example, is the distinction to be applied to a messenger's report in a play (a very common device)? By an act of reflection the reader may fit the events reported by the messenger into the order of occurrence, and we would then say that the order of presentation differs from the order of occurrence. Or, we may consider the messenger's entire narrative as an occurrence, and say that it is presented in the same order in which it occurs. Macduff tells Macbeth that he was from his mother's womb untimely ripped. Macduff's birth obviously occurred many years before the witches spoke in Act IV, scene i; but Macduff tells Macbeth about it just before their final duel and shortly after Birnam wood comes to Dunsinane, and the telling is itself a dramatic event.[10]

In novels, and to an even greater extent in motion pictures, the device known as the flashback is often used. Here, instead of a merely verbal narration by someone who knows about events long past, the old events are presented, out of their chronological order, by much the same mode of presentation used in the rest of the work: in a novel, after the narration has begun with events occurring, say, in May, 1934, a section may follow which narrates events supposed to have happened in January, 1902; and the same sort of thing is done in motion pictures, where the earlier events are not just presented in the words of one of the characters, but in pictures.[11] It is of elementary importance for the reader to keep clearly in mind these different kinds of order.

Once the various orders of events are determined, there are many questions which naturally arise, particularly if the order of the author's presentation differs from the understood order of occurrence. Actually, *Macbeth* presents comparatively few striking problems of this sort, because rarely in the play do the speakers refer to events already completed. They do however, make accurate prophecies about future events. But when the reader does encounter shifts in time sequence he should inquire about their

[10] Sophocles' *Oedipus the King* is a clearer example of this. In the course of the play the hero, Oedipus, discovers many things about his own life; but these discoveries are themselves events of the play and occur in the play in the same order they are understood to occur in chronologically, even though they concern things that happened years before Oedipus discovers them and so, considered in this way, their order of presentation is the same as their order of occurrence.

[11] Motion pictures sometimes combine a character's verbal account with a cinematographic representation, by having the character's voice describe and comment on the action while the moving pictures are presented. This is often done in cinema adaptations of novels written in the first person. The reader may find it interesting to reflect on this in connection with the remarks made below, pp. 91–97, on the function of the narrator. If the motion picture did not do this, it could lose precisely the effect the novelist sought in choosing to write in the first person.

effects. How, for example, do they affect feelings like that of suspense? Suspense may depend on delay in giving the reader information. If the hero is about to be overwhelmed, and help is two hours away, it might be best if we were not told, too soon, that the cavalry started to the rescue an hour and fifty-five minutes ago. And suspense is lost, to a certain extent, when the narration is given in the first person, since we know that the narrator has survived to tell the tale; there is a difference, however, if we know that he is the only survivor. And narration in the first person need not destroy our curiosity about the course of events, since we may still wonder how, precisely, the survivals or destructions took place; and our wonder may be increased by our feeling that survival seems impossible, although we know it has happened. We must remember, however, that such elements as suspense are only parts of the total effect of a work and that they must be artistically related to other parts if the work as a whole has an organic structure. The author cannot—without violating the structure of his work—introduce suspense-producing devices if these are out of harmony with any essential part of the whole. As a possible illustration, we might imagine that the weird sisters gave information to Macduff as well as Macbeth, in a version of *Macbeth* different from Shakespeare's. This could conceivably have interesting effects, but it would be hard to harmonize with Shakespeare's Macbeth, for it is peculiarly appropriate in that play for the witches to communicate with certain people and not with others. Again, in *The Odyssey*, Odysseus' manner of narrating his adventures in the court of the Phaeacians is not only characterized by a peculiar sort of excitement but is appropriate to the character of Odysseus.

We may also ask whether the significance of the narrated events is colored by the circumstances in which they are reported. We think events are significant, not simply because of what they are in themselves, but because of what they follow from and what they lead to. If the hero is fighting a duel, the fight itself may be full of interest. It will gain significance if we already know, before it begins, that the heroine is in danger, and that the hero must win the duel if he is to rescue her. Again, our coming to know a character makes a difference in the attitude we have toward what he tells us. By the time he tells of events long past, we may know that he is likely to exaggerate, or to tone down, his own role in those events; from our knowledge of his character we may even suspect that things were not at all as he says they were, and this suspicion may hearten or dishearten us, depending on the situation which prevails at the time of the narration.

Leaving now the question of time sequences, let us turn more directly to consider problems in terms of the particular sections into which plays or novels can be divided. Just what are the main divisions of the book, and how are these to be subdivided? Questions along this line come immediately to mind, and they can be of great importance. But they can hardly be answered until an interpretation has been pretty well worked out, and it is usually better to postpone them for a while, and to make simpler beginnings. Conventional divisions—acts, scenes, chapters, paragraphs, speeches, and so on—can be accepted at first. Or, the reader may try quite arbitrary divisions, reflecting upon them as he explores the questions they raise.

Let the reader begin by picking a small section, only large enough for something to happen in (even if he is unable to tell, at first, that something does indeed happen in it). Suppose he decides to examine the last scene of Act I in *Macbeth*. What happens in the scene? To whom does it happen? Whom else does it involve, and how? What happens is that Macbeth makes up his mind to murder Duncan, and Lady Macbeth formulates the general plan for the murder. The reader might be uncertain about this, wondering whether the chief happening in the scene is not the changing of Macbeth's mind, since he says in line 30: "We will proceed no further in this business." Or the reader may think that this line itself marks one change of Macbeth's mind and that he returns to his original intention when he says, in lines 79–80:

> I am settled, and bend up
> Each corporal agent to this terrible feat.

However the reader may decide this question, Macbeth does come to a decision, and the scene is concerned with his reaching it. Im-

74

portant questions have to do with the nature of the problem Macbeth faces in making the decision, and his reasons for making it. Why is it a difficult decision? Is Macbeth a coward, as Lady Macbeth suggests in line 43, or are we inclined to accept Macbeth's proudly indignant rejection of the suggestion?

> Prithee, peace!
> I dare do all that may become a man;
> Who dares do more is none.

This line of questioning should lead the reader to analyze the soliloquy which begins the scene. Is it not likely, since it is a soliloquy, to be a reliable indication of Macbeth's real attitudes? Lady Macbeth's remarks obviously have much to do with bringing about the ultimate decision; but it may be hard to find, in her words, really logical answers to the doubts expressed by Macbeth in the soliloquy. Consider that Lady Macbeth makes three main speeches in the scene. How do they differ? The first accuses Macbeth of cowardice. The second indirectly accuses him of irresolution, and perhaps of tenderness. The third considers the murder's chances of success and outlines a plan for bringing it off. At the end of the third speech Macbeth expresses enthusiasm for Lady Macbeth's undaunted mettle and makes his decision. How do these speeches persuade Macbeth to undertake the murder? When Lady Macbeth enters, at line 28, the two persons have different views of the murder, and at the end of the scene they have come to an agreement. But have they really come to view the murder in the same way? We know that Lady Macbeth did not hear Macbeth's soliloquy; so she has not heard his full expression of his view—she may, in fact, be incapable of understanding it, because of the kind of person she is. Does he, then, change his mind because she has resolved the doubts expressed in the soliloquy? Or, because she has brought him to see the enterprise in a new light? Must it not be the latter, since she does not speak at all to the moral considerations that are so prominent in his mind during the soliloquy? Apart from her influence he had not thought of the daring spirit that the murder called for. It was not that he was incapable of thinking of it, but that his mind dwelt instead upon the moral aspects of the contemplated deed. She, however, is so effective in what she emphasizes that she influences him to suppress his moral scruples in his admiration for her "undaunted mettle," for the spirit which lies back of the line; "Who dares receive it other?" When she suggests that Macbeth is cowardly, she is surely wide of the mark. Her words here irritate Macbeth. He retorts, "Prithee, peace." But the spirit she shows, when she speaks of cowardice, commands his admiration, and the traits in Macbeth that make him admire it must help him make the fatal decision.

Questions limited to what is going on within even one small scene may do much to enrich our understanding of the entire play. This scene helps us understand why both characters, Macbeth and Lady Macbeth, are necessary for the working-out of the action of this play, what the function of each is in this action, and how their different functions are related to each other. This mode of analysis can be developed, and understanding of the whole play enlarged, by asking how the events that occur in this scene follow from or lead to other events which occur in other scenes.

Several scenes should be considered. Since a good play or novel may be presumed to be well integrated, it does not matter very much what scenes or other parts are selected. Sequences of questions that arise from different starting points begin to cut across one another, as analysis proceeds. The reader might examine II, ii[12] (during which the murder of Duncan is accomplished), and the sleepwalking scene. In both these scenes, as well as in the one just discussed above, the reader might ask questions comparing the attitudes of the two leading characters toward the murder and other things related to it. In II, ii, the same sounds and sights provoke quite different reactions by Macbeth and by Lady Macbeth. He hears things which she does not hear; he entertains thoughts which she thinks "will make us mad"; Duncan's resemblance to her father prevents her killing him; Macbeth's imagining of the consequences of his act make him say,

---

[12] Large and small Roman numerals are used to refer to the act and scene, respectively. Thus, II, ii, 1-10, refers to lines one to ten of the second scene of the second act.

> I am afraid to think what I have done;
> Look on't again I dare not.

In reflecting on the sleepwalking scene, the reader will no doubt find himself trying to fit together the ideas that have come to him concerning all three of the scenes just discussed. It was Macbeth who feared the consequences of the murder, at the end of Act I and at the beginning of Act II,[13] but it is Lady Macbeth, in Act V, whose sleep is ruined. And their different remarks about their bloody hands, in Acts II and V, respectively, provoke comparison. Is Lady Macbeth's concern for the sight and smell of her hands, in Act V, consistent with her remarks in Act II? Would it seem right if Lady Macbeth's speech about bloody hands were made by Macbeth, and vice versa? And how do all such questions affect the reader's feelings about Macbeth before and after his ruin?

When the reader's questions about different sections of the play begin to relate more and more to one another, he has an indication that his analysis is approaching completeness.

Another mode of analysis differs, primarily in the character of its starting points, from that which has just been described. Instead of selecting a section that has some magnitude, the reader may choose something indivisible. A word or a term may sometimes provide a good starting point, or perhaps a line or a speech. Consideration of a single word quickly involves the reader in a consideration of the line to which it belongs and, after that, of the context in which the line appears. This mode of analysis characteristically proceeds to consider a small starting point in broader and broader contexts, until the whole play becomes the point of reference.

---

[13] I, vii, 1–4:
> "If it were done when 'tis done, then 'twere well
> It were done quickly. If the assassination
> Could trammel up the consequence, and catch
> With his surcease success; . . ."

And II, ii, 35–36:
> "Methought I heard a voice cry 'Sleep no more!
> Macbeth does murder sleep.' . . ."

For any term or line or speech, the reader should ask himself, What is the situation at this point in the play? He should follow by asking how this situation is colored by what the reader already knows. This question can, in some instances, introduce great complexities. What the reader already knows can, in second readings, or in dramatic presentations of familiar stories, include things that happen later in the play. If for any reason the reader knows more about the situation than one or more of the characters knows, the significance of this difference should be explored. How do the various characters feel about this situation? How does their limited knowledge of the situation affect the reader's feelings for these characters? Does it increase or lessen the reader's apprehensions, hopes, pity, or fear for these characters?

It is difficult to illustrate this mode of analysis, because, although several sorts of questions can be raised about almost any minute part, some of these questions will prove very important for some parts and comparatively unimportant for others. But let us take, for this kind of consideration, line 17, from V, v: "She should have died hereafter." At this point in the play Lady Macbeth's death has just been announced to Macbeth. He, deserted by most of his followers, is preparing desperately to resist an attack upon his castle. Combined armies from Scotland and England, led by men determined to wreak vengeance upon Macbeth for his many crimes, oppose him. Lady Macbeth's mind has been "diseased," apparently beyond cure. There are many such facts that Macbeth and the reader both know; if we have read the play before, we know, and Macbeth does not, that he himself has not long to live; he has, to be sure, made remarks which show that he fears the situation is hopeless.[14] He does not yet know, but the reader does, that he has misinterpreted the witches' prophecy about Birnam wood; the reader knows this even if he has not finished his first reading of the play and thus has more reason than Macbeth to believe that no charm is going to protect him.

---

[14] Consider his extreme nervous irritability in V, iii. He reminds himself of the charms the witches have promised him but seems to find little real comfort in this thought.

The reader may, in the context of his understanding of the situation, go on to ask what the line, "She should have died hereafter," means. We cannot be certain of the literal meaning in this case. It may mean, "It would have been better if she had died later"; or, it may mean, "If she had not died at this time, she would have died sooner or later anyhow." The first interpretation seems to be supported by the line which follows: "There would have been a time for such a word." For this sounds like an explanation: "She ought to have died later; it would then have been possible to give proper attention to the news of her death, and it is not possible now." But the reader may feel that the second interpretation, expressing something like indifference to the news, is more in keeping with the lines that begin, "Tomorrow, and tomorrow, and tomorrow." Still, these famous lines could very well follow, even according to the first interpretation, if we take into account Macbeth's state of mind at this time and what has happened to his character as his terrible career unfolded. A little earlier, in scene iii, his spirit has shifted rapidly from a mood of something like confidence, to deep despair. Could we interpret his reactions to the news of his wife's death after the same pattern? The first remark, "She should have died hereafter;/There would have been a time for such a word," could be said to reflect at least a little hope about the future: had she died hereafter, there would have been a time for such news, sad as it is, to be duly received; but the present offers no such time. This is far from cheerful thinking, but his mood becomes even darker as he reflects on his own thought about the future and the present: "Tomorrow, and tomorrow, and tomorrow." However we resolve this problem, we must come to a decision about Macbeth's frame of mind during the speech; and it is easy to broaden the context of our reflections by asking how he was brought to this frame of mind.

The process of broadening our inquiry should be systematic. If we ask how Macbeth reached the state of mind reflected in the "Tomorrow, and tomorrow" speech, it would not be enough to compare this state of mind with the one reflected in the soliloquy which begins in I, vii. Not that the present analysis should ignore

the earlier speech, but rather that the inquiry should try to connect the two states of mind, as well as all other states of mind, by
constructing a continuous history of the change in Macbeth's attitudes throughout the play. Do the various states of mind seem to
fall into an intelligible pattern? If so, or not, what seems to bring
them about at the points where they actually occur?

The mode of analysis now being considered can be further
illustrated in connection with another point in the text, the phrase
from I, iii, 141–42: "nothing is / But what is not." It is often
useful to select a phrase or term which puzzles the reader, at
least temporarily. Reflective reading may get special dividends
out of puzzling passages, because these are the very passages unreflective reading is likely to pass by, if it can. More puzzling
passages than the above can be found, to be sure; but this one does
seem deliberately enigmatic, self-contradictory. Here, matters do
not seem to be improved by considering a broader context, because
preceding lines, such as ". . . function / Is smothered in surmise,"
and, "My thought, whose murder yet is but fantastical," are not
themselves entirely clear.[15] But again, what is the situation? Macbeth is rapt. What about? He is reflecting on the fact that one of
the witches' prophecies has already been fulfilled. He does not
need Banquo's suggestion, although Banquo gives it to him any-
way, that the fulfillment of the prophecy encourages him to hope
for the crown. What are his thoughts about the crown? The crown
is the greatest of the promises; two truths told by the witches are
. . . happy prologues to the swelling act / Of the imperial theme."
He cannot decide that these ideas are either good or bad. The conclusion of the first stage of the inquiry (in which the phrase is considered in its immediate context) might be summarized as follows:
Macbeth finds himself yielding to his imagination's suggestion that
he murder Duncan; this thought grips him so powerfully that,

---

[15] Such difficult passages emphasize the need for dictionaries, glossaries,
editions with good footnotes, and so on, in the reading of writers like
Shakespeare, much of whose language is archaic. The puzzling lines just
quoted can help, if "function" and "fantastical" are properly understood.

although it is only imaginary, it seems to him the only real thing in the world. If the reader can provisionally accept this account of the meaning of the phrase, "nothing is / But what is not," he can proceed to use this meaning (and to test it) by seeing how it fits with what follows (here nothing much precedes it, since it occurs so near the beginning of the play and so near Macbeth's first appearance). This procedure should help the reader decide how far the murder of Duncan was Macbeth's own responsibility, and how far Lady Macbeth's, since the phrase in question occurs before, but shortly before, Lady Macbeth appears in the play. The decision will have an important bearing on the reader's interpretation of the play. At this point is Macbeth contented with his state of mind? Is he satisfied to accept what is not (the but imagined murder of Duncan and his own acquiring of the crown) for what is? Does he think he should do anything in order to make the imaginary situation an actual situation? Or does he think he should let the future unfold itself? And how are these questions related to the conversations between Macbeth and Lady Macbeth soon after this scene? How does she react to the same news (of Macbeth's new title, Thane of Cawdor)? Are not her words strikingly similar to his?

> Thy letters have transported me beyond
> This ignorant present, and I feel now
> The future in the instant.[16]

But is her state of mind as much like his as this similarity would, in itself, suggest? On the contrary, there is no thought at all of letting the future unfold itself. The death of Duncan must be "this night's great business."

A particular passage may serve as the point of departure for analysis, but the focus can be turned in quite a different direction by asking how the effect of the whole play would be altered if the passage in question were to appear in a different place, or were to be eliminated from the play altogether. Although such a question

---

[16] I, v, 57–59.

can be very helpful, it should be handled very cautiously; for it can reveal much more about some works than about others, as we shall see in our discussion of differences between the dramatic and the narrative manners of presentation.[17]

One more way of beginning an inquiry may be mentioned, although it can only be used by groups of readers. One person may read a line or a speech aloud and the others may criticize his reading. This procedure will emphasize the fact that the dramatic meaning of the words cannot be found in a merely literal interpretation; it is necessary for the reader to commit himself to some view of the state of mind of the character who is supposed to be speaking, for this commitment will determine whether such a line as "She should have died hereafter" should be read as an expression of annoyance, indifference, deep grief, or something else. Those who hear the reading will be able to imagine other ways to read the lines, and fruitful questions will arise about the dramatic appropriateness of one reading or another. Such a procedure could be used in the study of a history but is more useful in reading fiction. Also, it is more generally useful in the study of drama than in the study of novels and short stories, but it can also be used with the latter, particularly in passages of dialogue.

The reader should strive, in the final stages of analysis, to bring together all of the ideas his study has brought out. Those modes of analysis which tend to disregard the sections and subdivisions of the play and concentrate instead upon elements that cut across sectional divisions (elements such as action, character, thought, diction, and spectacle) will probably lead the reader to conclude that one of these elements is of central importance. Those modes of analysis which concentrate upon the sections or subdivisions will lead the reader to conclude that some dividing points are of special importance: he will gain confidence in deciding what the play's beginning, middle, and ending sections are. He will be able to mark the beginning or ending of a play only if he has a clear idea of what begins, and what ends, in the play. If, in *Macbeth*, he believes that

---

[17] See the discussion of the inclusion of comparatively unimportant things in long novels, below, pp. 97–98.

the play's central concern is the destruction of Macbeth's moral character, he might conclude that the play's beginning lasts until Macbeth says, in II, i, 63–64:

> Hear it not, Duncan; for it is a knell
> That summons thee to heaven, or to hell.

The middle of the play would then begin with II, ii, and the destruction of Macbeth's moral character could be considered complete, and the ending of the play to begin, with IV, i, 146, where Macbeth says:

> From this moment
> The very firstlings of my heart shall be
> The firstlings of my hand.[18]

When we use terms like *beginning, middle,* and *end,* we are referring to some kind of movement. It is useful, not only to ask about the beginning, middle, and ending sections, but also to try to determine the precise points at which the movement begins and ends. These considerations can help make clear just what kind of movement takes place in the work. And they may raise questions which otherwise might be overlooked: Why does the work include a part before the beginning of the movement, and why a part after the movement ends? Of *Macbeth* it could be said that the movement does not begin until some point after Macbeth's first entrance upon the stage and that the movement ends with his death (both of these statements could, of course, be disputed). If we do say this, what then do we say about the functions of those initial and concluding sections? An answer might be found along the following lines. These two parts of the play provide a context within which the central movement of the play takes place, and thus add to the significance of the movement. Before Macbeth enters, the play presents us with a political situation

---

[18] It would require a good deal of space to defend such conclusions; the reader is not expected to accept them at face value. It should be kept in mind, however, that the accepted divisions of Shakespeare's plays into acts and scenes were supplied by editors, not by Shakespeare himself.

which has just been stabilized after a period of conflict; and Macbeth has been instrumental in establishing this stability. After Macbeth dies, the play again presents us with a political situation which has just been stabilized after a period of conflict: but Macbeth has not been instrumental in establishing this stability—in fact, it is he who has been the cause of the conflict. The central movement could be regarded as one that led from the first period of stability to the second. No interpretation of the play would be adequate if it left this out of account.[19]

There are two aspects of drama that have received little attention thus far: its actual language (diction), and how things look on the stage (spectacle). Analysis can find good points of departure, and interpretations can find good tests, in either of these. Spectacle will be briefly considered below, in the discussion of dramatic and narrative manners of presentation. A few remarks here about diction may be helpful.

Diction is manifestly important in drama, since we could say that a play is made primarily out of spoken words. Language, however, has such power to attract attention to itself that it may, in large works, distract the reader's attention from matters essential to the work as a whole. Shakespeare is the most quoted of all English authors, and when fragments from his plays are quoted, their complete dramatic contexts are usually ignored. No fault need be found with this manner of quoting; it is only mentioned here to demonstrate that the poetry of small passages of Shakespeare (or of other writers) is in itself very striking, so much so that it can be appreciated without regard to its full context. The reader whose primary aim is to gain an understanding of a play as a whole should be able to account for the dramatist's use of lyrical effects (or of prosaic effects), as well as for other details of diction. And he can

---

[19] It is interesting to compare plays in this respect. In *Macbeth* the curtain falls soon after Macbeth's death. In Sophocles' *Oedipus the King* much more time elapses between the terrible catastrophe which Oedipus suffers and the very end of the play. These final sections must function in very different ways in the two plays. The difference could be described by saying that the resolution of *Macbeth* is sudden, but the resolution of *Oedipus the King* is much more gradual.

use these effects analytically, in his effort to come to an interpretation of the whole. The dramatic effects of diction are very
rich in variety, and one should be cautious about generalizing. Still,
for convenience, several kinds of effects can be pointed out. These
are only suggestive of the enormous variety that exist, especially
if possible permutations and combinations are taken into account.

How do the large sections of blank verse, or the sections of
prose, affect the reader's feelings about what he reads? In general
prose is less serious in tone than verse (there are notable exceptions); and some kinds of verse are more lofty and more moving
than others.[20] Deliberately incongruous use of various forms of
diction may have a variety of possible effects. Satire often employs
a lofty diction in giving an account of a base or ridiculous matter;
or, the other way around, a serious matter can be effectively presented in very simple language, the combination producing a very
special effect. The reader should be alert for such twists. *Macbeth*
may not seem to provide many examples of this use of diction. But
what of the Porter's speech about the knocking at the gate at the
beginning of II, iii? This is surely humorous and base in its diction,
but how does the reader react to the diction in the context of the
play? Is he not still moved by the effects of the murder scene?
Doesn't the continuation of the knocking, which began during the
preceding scene and which punctuates the Porter's remarks, keep
the whole context in the reader's mind? And if the reader was apprehensive at the close of the preceding scene, doesn't the rhythmic
character of the knocking itself contribute to the reader's feeling
of nervousness? If these things are possible, one may hesitate to
conclude that the Porter's scene is simply funny; its effect may be
quite the reverse.

The expressive quality of a particular passage may function in
a variety of ways. At one extreme it may be separable from the situation in which it occurs, and from the character who speaks the

---

[20] Even in plays which do not use verse, something of the same kinds of
difference can often be found. In Shakespeare, some of the differences are
better exemplified in plays which contain more comic sections than *Macbeth*,
e.g., *King Henry IV*, Parts I and II.

lines. The moving (or, in comedy, witty) expression of a universal truth, may have as its background the whole play, or life in general, rather than just one of the play's situations or characters. At another extreme, what is said may be significant because of that which it contributes to the reader's understanding of a particular situation or character. The reader should therefore ask himself, for any emphatically poetic passage, which sort of significance it has in the play. Macbeth's "Tomorrow, and tomorrow" speech seems, because it is an eloquent statement about life in general, to be close to the first extreme, and perhaps based on something more general than the particular character of Macbeth, or the situation in which he speaks. On the other hand, his earlier speech,

> My way of life
> Is fall'n into the sear, the yellow leaf,

is more obviously one that refers to a particular character, Macbeth himself, in a particular situation. Still, the reader should be cautious about taking, as an expression of the heart of the play, the lines:

> . . . life . . . is a tale
> Told by an idiot, full of sound and fury,
> Signifying nothing.

This speech, however universal in its intended application, must be understood as coming from the man Macbeth, and it is even significant that it comes later than the "sear, the yellow leaf" speech.

On this point, as always, the reader should be on his guard against oversimplification. He should not expect that any given passage will have only one kind of significance. The very fact that a passage seems richly significant outside its context presents a kind of danger: the reader may accept that significance, without diligently seeking the significance of the passage in its context. The "Tomorrow, and tomorrow, and tomorrow" passage is a good illustration, for it would be a mistake to be too impressed by the significance it has in itself, if we are prevented as a result from inquiring into the function of the speech in the play as a whole.

There are many ways in which an emphatically poetic passage can contribute to the reader's understanding of a particular situation or character. We shall consider one especially important way. Let us note that one does not understand whole plays or their parts merely by learning the facts; we understand dramatic characters and their actions as we understand people, and in both cases much depends upon our ability to share their feelings. Because poetry is so effective a means of communicating feelings, the poetic diction of a drama can add to the reader's understanding of dramatic parts and wholes, can add, that is, something beyond mere information. The reader can therefore ask, about any particular passage, how it affects him beyond giving him the information that a merely literal interpretation of the words would give. Take the two speeches we were just considering. The "Tomorrow, and tomorrow" speech can be considered literally as an expression of despair and of a feeling of utter futility. But, as Shakespeare gives it to us, does not the passage have a poetic beauty that suggests the speaker to be a man brought to this state of mind only after he has been something quite different? And doesn't an adequate appreciation of the passage's poetry affect our attitude toward Macbeth and his fate? Two similar questions can be asked about the other speech. (How does the diction enrich our understanding of the lines? Does this enrichment affect our attitude toward the speaker and his situation?) Even more clearly, perhaps, "My way of life" suggests, in spite of its despairing quality, a speaker with a deep appreciation of the values that should accompany old age; and we are moved by this, not as we would be moved by a man who was merely lamenting a fate which is, after all, richly deserved. Further, if we take the two speeches together, remembering which occurs first in the play, does the poetic expression help us to see a change going on in the inner character of Macbeth? The bitterness is deeper in the second speech and applies to all life, not just to Macbeth's present way of life.

Striking features of diction occur not only in particular passages of a play or novel; several passages may together make up a pattern of imagery which runs through the play as a whole. Essays have been written pointing out that *Macbeth* repeatedly employs images based upon the idea of garments, and the ways in which they fit or do not fit; or images which emphasize contrasts between light and darkness. One critic has called *Macbeth* "the tragedy of the twilight and the setting-in of thick darkness upon a human soul," and suggests as a "motto of the entire tragedy," the line from III, ii: "Good things of day begin to droop and drowse."[21] Such patterns can be found, but much effort in this direction is not recommended here. Pervasive effects of diction work upon the reader, no doubt, but probably in a rather subtle fashion which the general reader does not especially need to be conscious of. Whenever a work is unified in terms of action or character its unity must be grasped in these terms; this should be the reader's first concern, and he should consider the effects of diction as they are related to that fundamental unity.

II

Most of the questions and procedures which have been suggested for the reading of drama could, with some modification, be employed also in the reading of narratives. The distance which separates drama from narrative is variable, since each makes use, in some way, of devices ordinarily associated with the other. Still, certain elements tend to be emphasized in dramatic structure, and others in narrative structure. Attention will now be given to some problems which are met with in the reading of drama more commonly than in the reading of narratives.

Special Problems in Reading Dramatic Literature

Dramas are, of course, intended for the stage, and although they can produce their effects without being represented on the stage, the reader should always try to visualize the staged play. Shake-

---

21 Edward Dowden, *Shakspere—His Mind and Art* (New York: Harper & Bros., 1918), p. 217.

speare's plays, and some others, give very few explicit directions about stage appearances and business. The reader whose habits encourage him to read everything as though it were not dramatic (in the theatrical sense of the word) is likely to hurry through the words and to be reluctant to take the time to visualize, or to imagine the pauses which are often essential to the dramatic effect of the scene. It is not that elaborate stage settings need always be imagined—sometimes it is quite the contrary, where a bleak or severe effect is called for.[22] But the reader should ask himself continually if there is something about the spectacle that is essential or important for the scene. The person who merely reads *Hamlet* (or, for that matter, one who sees a black and white motion picture of it) misses something if he fails to imagine the effect made by the fact that Hamlet's "inky cloak" stands out against a crowd of people dressed in bright colors, as the second scene opens. The banquet scene in *Macbeth* loses much of its effect if the reader forgets that there are persons present who are not speaking, persons whose reaction to the ghost of Banquo is totally different from Macbeth's reaction, but who must indicate to the eye their astonishment at Macbeth's behavior. Brief stage directions, like "They fight," are in themselves inadequate indications of many stage combats, if these combats are to live up to the demands of their full dramatic contexts. Laughs are an important aim of many comedies. They are produced sometimes by jokes, sometimes by ludicrous situations. The humor may not be apparent if the reader does not imagine little pieces of stage business, or if he does not properly imagine the pace at which the lines are delivered—a joke may be very funny if it is timed well, but fall flat if it is not.

It is easy for the reader to overlook important dramatic pauses. In the banquet scene in *Macbeth* the reader must imagine an awkward pause when Macbeth is unable to find a place at the table because Banquo's ghost is sitting there. And the text suggests another awkward pause toward the end of the scene, when Lady

---

[22] Productions of Shakespeare's plays, as well as of other dramas, can be effective with little or no scenery—as they were produced in Shakespeare's day.

Macbeth hurries the guests by saying, "Stand not upon the order of your going." When Macduff hears of the slaughter of his family, Malcolm says to him:

> What, man! Ne'er pull your hat upon your brows,
> Give sorrow words. The grief that does not speak
> Whispers the o'erfraught heart and bids it break.[23]

This speech makes little sense unless the reader vividly imagines Macduff's stage behavior. There must be, throughout this scene, painful pauses during which the other characters stand speechless. Notice how often Macduff asks questions whose answers he has already been told. How would the effect of the scene change if fairly long pauses were not made before each of these questions?

Plays have some features that are simply imposed upon them by the conditions of staging. The reader should continually ask himself what these features are. Sometimes it is necessary to be aware of them to keep from giving them undue importance. By the end of the second scene of *Macbeth*, for example, the bleeding sergeant has spoken more than any other character. But there is no reason to assume that he is to be an important character in the play, as a character; he is merely fulfilling a function not uncommon in plays: giving the audience, in a convenient way, information about the leading character before the playwright wishes that character to appear upon the stage. The first entrance of the hero can often be more dramatic, theatrically, if the audience knows something about him before he appears. In rearranging his stage the playwright may, for example, have to call for a number of entrances and exits, and these may be more obtrusive on the stage than he would wish (the novelist's problem is usually simpler in this respect). But the skillful writer can make these necessities unobtrusive, or he may even make dramatic capital out of them. In Shakespeare the actual scene of action seems to shift very little; the space represented on the stage often remains the same in different "scenes," and the actors take turns in occupying it (just as they take turns in occupying the stage itself). These features were dic-

---

[23] IV, iii, 208–10.

tated by stage practices of Shakespeare's time, and they probably disturb very few spectators or readers, even though reflection might make it seem improbable that all the important personal combats of a battle could take place on one little spot in a large battlefield. In fact, such stage conditions are typical of limitations that encourage the dramatist to work for effects whose peculiar power derives from the economy of means used to produce them. The comparatively small number of fully drawn characters and the comparatively simple action of *Macbeth* enable Shakespeare to explore in a very special way the inner struggles of Macbeth and Lady Macbeth and their interrelationships.

Special Problems in Reading Narrative Literature

Some of the special problems in reading narrative literature can be understood if we begin with a working hypothesis: the essential difference between novels and plays involves the function of the narrator. This can only be a working hypothesis, because we should not be able to find any works which were pure examples of what we call *narratives* or *dramas*. We shall think, rather, of what we may call narrative or dramatic *manner*, recognizing that elements of dramatic manner can be found in novels, and elements of narrative manner in plays.

Let us say that a work is dramatic in manner precisely to the extent that we (the readers or spectators) seem to see things directly, that is, without having them presented to us through some mediator. And let us say that a work is narrative in manner precisely to the extent that what we experience, in the work, could only be experienced indirectly, that is, through the mediation of a narrator. A theatrical presentation comes close to being something that we see with our own eyes, without anyone's help. Whenever we know that we are hearing or reading a narration, however, we are aware of the presence of the narrator and know that we depend upon him for experiencing the things he talks about. A few considerations will show us that the two manners are not in fact sharply separated.

First, anything that happens differently on the stage from the way things happen in ordinary life can call our attention to the fact that what we see and hear is being controlled by someone other than ourselves; this other person must be regarded, according to our working hypothesis, as a narrator. Whenever a dramatic action is interrupted, say, by a change of scene, what we see or hear is being arranged for us by a narrator; whenever the action on the stage does not follow the ordinary flow of time (time can move backwards in literature, or great chunks of it can be skipped over), someone else is arranging things for us. Again, if we are permitted, by means of soliloquy or by other unrealistically intimate revelations, to see what is going on "inside" a character, we are seeing something that we cannot actually see in ordinary life. All such things, even when they occur in plays, are narrative in manner, according to our hypothesis. The very processes of analytic reflection may call our attention to the existence of a narrator, when we study plays, although in the theater itself we may "lose ourselves" in the presentation. In dramas, more than in novels, we tend to identify the narrator with the author. In reflection we may find ourselves saying, "Shakespeare presents Macbeth and Lady Macbeth as characters who share a goal, but who do not understand that goal in the same way." Still, the activity of the narrator is not typically so apparent in plays as in novels.

Second, in many novels and short stories a sense of immediate presentation is an important part of good writing, and immediateness is particularly characteristic of the dramatic manner. We can distinguish degrees of immediateness in our understanding of various characters in narratives. A high degree of immediateness can be achieved when the situations, characters, and actions of the book are presented through the eyes of one of the characters. The feeling of immediateness requires that our point of view be identified with that character's point of view. To the extent that this identification occurs, it does not seem that we are *told* what happens; instead we seem to *see* everything as the character would immediately see it. The effect is strengthened if his innermost thoughts and feelings are revealed to us, probably because, in real life, we know no one except ourselves so intimately.

What happens if the reader is given the same intimate under-standing of many—perhaps all—of the characters? This has been often attempted, and the effect is complex. To a certain extent such a book becomes dramatic in manner, because all the characters are presented to us in the same way—we identify ourselves with no one character more than another. But in other ways the effect is non-dramatic, because the dramatic manner does not give us oppor-tunity for an intimate identification with any one character. There are literary works to which our distinction between dramatic and narrative manner cannot be clearly applied. Good writers have probably tried to break it down, in order to achieve effects that are impossible with either a simple dramatic or narrative manner.

The effect of immediacy depends upon another factor, already commented upon: the extent to which we let the work have its way with us, and the extent to which we analyze and reflect upon it. When, for example, the characters and situations in a piece of literature seem to be as vividly presented to us as the persons and situations of our everyday experience (and this could result from a mode of presentation which does not reveal innermost thoughts and feelings), we may almost lose ourselves in the work. When we do this, our reactions to the work are immediate, and the work tends to become dramatic; when we reflect upon a work we be-come more conscious of the function of the narrator, who is never altogether absent from any work of drama or fiction. There are narrative writings which do not encourage the reader to identify himself with any of the characters. This is often true of passages which consist chiefly of dialogue, and also, although to a lesser ex-tent, of unembellished accounts of overt actions (like vivid news-paper reporting). Nevertheless, such passages can be dramatic in manner, as is testified to by the fact that they are readily adapted for performance on the stage.

In novels it is of more pressing importance than in plays to understand the character of the narrators. The reader should put aside any tendency to identify the narrator with the person of the author who wrote the book. The tendency need not be rejected completely, although the suggestions in this chapter are based on the conviction that all narrators are separable from the persons who write the books. This thesis will be in part justified by the considerations here put forward concerning narrators; to defend it in full is beyond the scope of this book. The reader should remember that to consider the narrator (that narrator who is most easily confused with the author) as though he were the author can be tantamount to forgetting that the author is an artist, and that his work is not a natural product of his personality.[24] Besides, it is characteristic of narrators to claim knowledge of sorts that no ordinary human being can really have. Some illustrations will show why it is reasonable to avoid identifying the narrator with the author.

First, consider *Treasure Island*. The reader would obviously make a mistake if he identified Jim Hawkins, who tells the story in the first person, with Robert Louis Stevenson, the author of the book. Jim stands between the reader and the events and conversations he describes; someone else stands between the reader and Jim. Second, consider *Lord Jim*. In this novel many characters, including Jim, the French naval officer, Stein, and Brown, present narrations. Between narrations and the reader stands another character, Marlow, through whom most of the story is passed on to the audience. Marlow does not merely hand on the narrations made by other characters; he does some narrating in his own person. Between Marlow and the reader stands someone else, who is the narrator of the book as a whole; Marlow's words are placed within quotation marks.[25] All that we know about Jim Hawkins we know from *Treasure Island*. All that we know of Marlow we know from *Lord Jim* and the other Conrad novels in which he appears. All that

---

[24] The idea that a narrator cannot simply be presumed to have the artistry of a novelist is reflected in the existence of some novels, for example, Laurence Sterne's *Tristram Shandy*, and—in our own day—John Barth's *The Floating Opera*, in which the narrator is expressly presented as the writer of a book, the very book in which he is the narrator. So, a narrator should not be regarded as an author, unless the book's author makes him one.

[25] A reader not familiar with this novel can get some idea of its complexity, in this respect, merely by glancing through it and observing the many quotations included within other quotations.

we know about the narrator who stands between us and Jim Hawkins, or the narrator who stands between us and Marlow, we learn from *Treasure Island* or from the novels of Conrad. The reader has no justification for assuming that Stevenson or Conrad, with their personal idiosyncrasies, are to be identified with the narrators in their novels. It is quite possible that these narrators are intended by their creators to be wiser, more penetrating in their insight, than the authors themselves. And there are certainly cases (like Ring Lardner's "Haircut") where the narrator is obviously stupid or obtuse.[26]

The problems which are special to the disciplines of reading narrative literature are, for the most part, consequences of the function of the narrator, and of the fact that the reader's mind, as he sits in his armchair, is freed from some of the limitations that are imposed upon the spectator of a play. We will not go into detail to suggest the questions which arise in connection with these problems; rather we will point out some of the features that are more likely to attain prominence in novels than in plays, because of the special character of the narrator and of the peculiar conditions of stage representation. And we will recommend that the reader be especially alert for these features, and for the effects which can follow when a narrative writer focuses attention upon them.

A narration is not limited, as dramatic representation characteristically is, to presenting overt actions and spoken or supposedly spoken words. The narrator may therefore emphasize other kinds of things: he may present the unexpressed thoughts of characters, he may psychoanalyze them, or he may show us objects, characters, situations, and events as these appear through the eyes of given

---

[26] There is an obverse side to this separation of the narrator and the author; the persons to whom the narrative is addressed are not simply identified with the actual readers of these books. This is made explicit in *Lord Jim*, where those who listen to Marlow talk are specified, although very vaguely, as sitting around after dinner, smoking cigars; and one of these listeners follows up Marlow's narrative by reading a letter many years later. The effect of these separations is to set the presentation and reception of the story apart from the idiosyncrasies of the particular men who write and read them. The separation exists even when it is not made so explicit as in *Lord Jim*.

characters; he may present all of these from a variety of definitely specified points of view (as he does in *Lord Jim*); he may take great liberties with the normal flow of time, and he may shift the focus of the reader's attention suddenly from one scene to another many miles away.[27]

Since the writer of narratives can present such things more readily than the dramatist, he is able to develop longer and more complex actions. His ability to do this is extended by the reader's willingness to undertake a book which he does not expect to finish reading in a single sitting—or even in a whole day's reading.[28] The reader, unlike the spectator of the drama, is also able to pause in his reading, and to reflect; he may even reread some passages before passing on to others. The apprehending of a narrative is so different from the watching of a dramatic action that long lists, catalogues (as in the *Iliad*), extremely detailed descriptions, long series of conversations—often about matters that have very little to do with moving the story along—come naturally from the pen of a narrative writer. It is possible therefore for him to form structures distinctively different from characteristically dramatic structures. The reader should ask questions about the non-dramatic elements of what he reads. If the role of narrator is assigned to a character, or if it is shifted now and then from one character to another, or to someone between the reader and all the characters, the reader should ask whether this manner of writing focuses his attention upon specific elements in the narrative; and he should consider these elements as points of departure for lines of questioning

[27] It must be kept in mind that all these things can be done in plays, by means of devices which have been used by dramatists for hundreds of years. But according to our hypothesis plays become narrative in their manner precisely to the extent that they employ such devices. In ordinary life it is perfectly natural for a narrator to do these things, whereas some convention must often be accepted if they are to be done on the stage. We take it as a matter of course, for example, if a friend tells us, "Before that happened I had lived for several years in New York, where . . ."

[28] The co-operation of the reader also makes it possible for the narrative writer to tell shorter stories than the dramatist. It hardly seems worthwhile to go to the theater for a very short play, and short plays are seldom staged.

analogous to those described in the discussion of *Macbeth*. Perhaps the most important question he should raise is this: With what person or persons do I tend to identify myself and my feelings? The immediateness of dramatic representation encourages the reader or spectator to identify himself with one or more of the play's characters. On the other hand, it is generally easier for the reader of narratives to identify himself with the narrator, whoever he may be, rather than with the characters he presents.[29]

Detailed descriptions and repeated and lengthy conversations are likely to present special problems to the reader of narratives. Two opposite kinds of errors can be made in reading descriptions. First, the reader may give them too much importance. The novelist may actually be resorting to description because it is his only means for doing what the dramatist can do in a few seconds with the stage spectacle.[30] Or, descriptions may be instances of a sort of lavish expenditure which the novelist can afford, whereas the dramatist must be more economical. Such lavish expenditure need not necessarily be wasteful. On the contrary, there are wonderful effects that can be produced only in this way. Even so, these wonderful effects may be the product of the sum of a great many details, and no single detail would have very much importance in itself. A similar effect may be produced by extensive use of conversations, especially if they appear to deal with somewhat trivial matters. Economy compels the dramatist to make each line of

---

[29] Let it be emphasized that the reader's identification with or separation from characters in a play or novel is a very complicated affair, about which it is very difficult to make general statements. When we react immediately to a work (and we have called this sort of reaction "losing ourselves in the work") we are prone to identify ourselves with one or more of the characters; when we reflect upon a work we are more apt to detach ourselves from all the characters. From the point of view of this book intelligent reading should not be reduced either to immediate apprehension or reflection: both are essential. We cannot, therefore, conclude that the sort of identification that goes along with losing ourselves in the work is more or less proper than that which goes along with reflection.

[30] Dramatists, of course, vary a great deal in the amount that they leave to stage directors in this matter.

dialogue carry a good deal of importance. The novelist, however, can more easily reproduce the vast amount of time human beings actually spend doing and talking about things that do not matter very much. One characteristic effect of the long novel, which is related to all of these matters, is the effect of making the reader feel that he is living for a considerable length of time in another world. The pace with which time moves on the stage does not permit this. And the larger role which unimportant details can play in novels is very much like life and helps make our experience of the novel like living in a world, a world we might have belonged to ourselves, except for the accidents of birth and fortune.

It is obviously wrong, also, to give too little importance to seemingly trivial details—to assume that detailed descriptions are only the novelist's clumsy way of doing what stage spectacles do so readily, and that the trivial things described and discussed in conversations are of little significance in the narrative, just because their subject matter is trivial. To a certain extent there is really no problem here for the reader. The effects of such passages are subtle and cumulative; the reader may not notice them, but they do build up in his mind, and color all his reading as the novelist wishes them to (if the reader really reads them), even if the reader does not reflect upon them. Still, it is prudent to ask what the possible effects of such accumulations are, in order to make sure not to ignore them. In this, as in other ways, it is good to follow the principle that books whose merit is generally recognized do not contain superfluous elements. Comparison of novels and plays can lead the reader to supplement this principle with another: different manners of presentation can affect the manner in which details become important, as they fit together to make up a whole literary structure.

Chapter 4

Philosophy

Like other literature, philosophy should be given a preliminary reading during which the reader does not pause for much reflection, even though such reading is especially difficult in philosophy.[1] A good playwright designs his drama so that it can be understood, at least up to a point, in a performance which takes only a few hours and which allows the spectator little time for reflection. In general, one can read fiction much more rapidly than philosophy. Philosophy characteristically expects the reader to think actively every step of the way, often to meditate; this involves reflection and takes time. In Descartes's *Meditations*, for example, each of the six meditations is regarded as requiring one day's thought, even though each meditation contains only a few words. Moreover, the book was originally published with a set of objections written by eminent contemporary thinkers, together with Descartes's replies to those objections. The objections and Descartes's replies to them are themselves reflections, and Descartes wanted them to be reflected on, in turn, by his readers.

In philosophical writing, more, say, than in drama, the small parts are likely to be problematic, at least on first acquaintance. Some single lines or words of a drama can, of course, present difficult problems of interpretation, but most of them are easy enough for the reader to accept on his first reading. With philosophy, however, the reader must be cautious from the outset about accepting what the smallest parts of the writing say. First, many of these parts

---

[1] This chapter is intended to be read along with Hume's *An Inquiry concerning the Principles of Morals*, the first half of Plato's *Meno*, and Section I of Part One of Dewey's *Human Nature and Conduct*.

are *prima facie* problematic; one has to think a bit before accepting them. Second, other parts that do not seem problematic lead to, or help lead to, conclusions that the reader may find it hard indeed to accept.[2] When this happens he may feel that he has been trapped, that he may have accepted something too easily, since he has been led to consequences he ought to accept but wishes to resist.

Because of the special difficulties in reading philosophy "straight through" we have to make a special effort. Two suggestions may help. First, on the preliminary reading accept what the author says provisionally, as though to say, "I will for the present consider that this statement may be true, and I will see where it leads." Second, mark any passages one has doubts about.[3]

What should the reader be on the alert for in his first reading of a work in philosophy? First, he should be seeking to arrive at a summary view of the work as a whole, analogous to the view expressed above (on p. 55) about *Macbeth*. If the work is as long as *Macbeth*, the expression of this summary view in writing (and it should be written when the first reading has been finished) will probably be more difficult to formulate than in *Macbeth*. Nevertheless, an initial reading straight through and a written summary should be attempted, even if the book is as long and as formidable

---

[2] We may note here a feature of philosophical reading that distinguishes it from the reading of drama or fiction. We expect that we should accept or reject what we encounter in philosophy. In imaginative literature we are not really called upon to commit ourselves in the same way.

[3] The reader will find it helpful to work out his own system of marginal notation (he should get inexpensive editions whenever possible, so that he will not hesitate to mark the books). One device may be suggested: the question mark may be used to mean various things, depending upon its position: in its normal position it may simply mean, "I don't quite understand what is meant here" (it is essential, in the interest of reading straight through, to pass by many such puzzling passages, the first time, but to be sure to return to them later); if the mark is placed in the margin upside down it can mean, "I think I understand this, but I challenge it"; other shades of the reader's reactions may be indicated by the two horizontal positions of the question mark. Other marks, such as the exclamation point, are also possible for recording one's reactions, but it is best if the reader does his marking in some systematic way.

as Kant's *Critique of Pure Reason*. The summary should attempt to state the main problem that the author is concerned with, and the conclusion he reaches. It may be that no solution is reached; the author's conclusion may then be that the problem cannot be solved (if so, he will probably indicate why).

Second, the reader's search for the main problem and the ultimate conclusion cannot be carried on effectively unless he is alert for the main terms, distinctions, and relations of the work. Although it may not be hard to discover the main terms, the reader must deliberately do this. At first one must watch for terms that are frequently repeated or that are given emphasis in some special way. The search for basic terms is closely bound up with concern for distinctions and relations. A term can hardly take on a meaning unless it is distinguished from other terms, and the practice of drawing distinctions has always been particularly characteristic of philosophers. Relations (or connections) are counterparts of distinctions (or separations), and accordingly contribute much to the meaning of the terms they involve. The philosophical importance of distinguishing and relating is indicated by St. Augustine's definition of reason as "a motion of the mind capable of differentiating and connecting the things which are learned."[4]

Third, as the reader goes through his first reading, alert for basic terms, distinctions, and relations, he should determine the relation of the parts (chapters, sections, paragraphs, and so on) both to one another and to the central problem.

Since such suggestions should be more meaningful in the concrete than in the abstract, we shall turn now to the examination of a particular work, David Hume's *An Inquiry concerning the Principles of Morals*.[5]

---

[4] *De ordine* I. xi, unpublished translation by Richard P. McKeon, University of Chicago.

[5] It is recommended that the reader have at his side, as he reads this chapter, an inexpensive edition of the *Inquiry*. Section numbers are the same in the various editions. Page numbers given here refer to the Library of Liberal Arts edition (New York, 1957).

I

Because of the difficulty of working out a preliminary summary statement of a work of philosophy, the reader must pay special attention to any clues that the author may give him concerning the nature of his problem, his terms, or his principles. The title itself, such as *An Inquiry concerning the Principles of Morals*, may be significant. Also, as in Hume's work, chapter headings and their arrangement in a table of contents give the reader a great deal of help in the third task mentioned above: working out an outline which shows how the parts are related to one another and to the whole.[6] Other clues that are sometimes given outside the body of the text, clues that should be noticed at the outset, include such aids as epigraphs, synopses, and marginal summaries of paragraphs (these, for example, are used by Kant, Descartes, and Locke, respectively). Readers should make sure that these were provided by the author himself.

Many books, including Hume's *Inquiry*, contain clear indications that the opening pages are introductory. Any introductory pages should be read with considerable care, even on the first reading. In the *Inquiry* Hume concludes Section I by saying, "we shall begin our inquiry on this head by the consideration of the social virtues; Benevolence and Justice. The explication of them will probably give us an opening by which the others may be accounted for."[7] This statement, along with others in Section I, and with the table of contents, suggests that Sections II through VIII constitute one inquiry, or two very closely related inquiries. Sec-

[6] I have thought it useful to pick a work that offers many such helps to the reader, even though so many other philosophical writings do not. We can save time and space by taking full advantage of what Hume has done for us and use his outline as a model of what the reader should work out for himself when the author does not provide one. In Hume's book it is interesting to notice that the classification of "mental qualities" made clear in the table of contents is kept in the background, in the body of the text, until very late in the book.

[7] In order to avoid an unnecessary proliferation of footnotes, page references to the text will not be given where the relevant passage can be readily found without them.

tion IX, "Conclusion," may be the conclusion to Sections II through VIII, or to the entire *Inquiry*, including Section I. We shall treat Section I as introductory, and ask how it can guide us in our approach to the rest of the book.[8] In particular, what guidance does Section I give for determining the main problem of the book, its principal terms, its distinctions and principles?

Section I does give useful answers to the questions we have proposed for the initial stages of our reading. The problem and the method of the inquiry are expressly discussed. The discussion proceeds by considering various alternatives. One controversy, concerning the reality of moral distinctions, is expressly rejected as the inquiry's problem. A second, whether morals be derived from reason or sentiment, is not simply rejected, but deferred. A third problem, to discover the true origin of morals, seems to be designated as the main problem of the inquiry.

The reader should at the very least take notice here of the fact that Hume formulates three problems he considers distinct. How they differ from one another can hardly be understood without a good deal of reflection, especially on the meanings of some of the terms. What is meant by *morals* or by *principles?* What could be meant by denying the reality of moral *distinctions?* What is the difference between asking whether morals are derived from reason or sentiment, and asking what the true origin of morals is?

The mere fact that Hume mentions problems he does not mean to discuss is no reason why the reader should ignore them, especially if he expects Section I to give him guidance during his first reading of the main part of the text. The number of problems that are not the subject of any given inquiry is infinite; Hume must have some reason for mentioning the two that he does.

A brief consideration of the first two questions (that are not to be Hume's subject) suggests something else that the reader of philosophy should be alert for, that is, controversies; Hume even calls these questions controversies. It helps to consider what posi-

---

[8] In addition to the nine sections into which the book is divided there are four appendixes, and a supplementary dialogue which Hume published with the *Inquiry*. There seem to be good reasons for considering the nine sections a complete book, without the appendixes and dialogue.

tions the author may be opposing, even though we are not conducting a historical study of Hume.[9] Even on first reading we may suspect that Hume intends eventually to give some attention to the view that denies the reality of moral distinctions, although he here presents the view as one which no reasonable man can or does actually hold. And the sheer amount of space devoted to the reason versus sentiment controversy (it gets seven of the eleven paragraphs in the section) bids us take it seriously, at least eventually, even if not on first reading.

It is to be expected that the student will examine the table of contents before moving on to Section II; for by this time he will have been told enough about the objective of the inquiry to make him wonder how it is going to be organized, and the table of contents is a good source of information about that. The table tells us that two of the appendixes are devoted to the questions of moral sentiment and of self-love. A footnote in Section I tells us that the former (which is expressly deferred in Section I, as a question easily answered when the real problem of the *Inquiry* has been resolved) is dealt with in Appendix I. We may well wonder whether the first controversy (concerning the reality of moral distinctions) is similarly dealt with; there is another reason for this wonder in the fact that the self-love issue appears to be of considerable importance in this book; so—on second reading, at least—one might wonder whether it does not appear, perhaps disguised, in Section I. It may be, then, that the first controversy is treated at length in Appendix II, on self-love.

The reader should see at this point that Hume views the reason versus sentiment controversy as one that is most properly settled after another problem has been examined. Yet, why does he devote so much space to the second controversy here? He takes the space to give arguments on both sides, and they are persuasive. They lead, however, only to a probable conclusion in favor of sentiment. This probable and provisional solution is confirmed in the sequel, but

[9] Our analysis here is not historical. But even when one is trying to analyze a work in its own terms, his alertness to controversies that play a part in that work may depend very much on the extent of his experience in philosophical reading.

with something better than the degree of probability reached in Section I.

Careful attention should be given to the long penultimate paragraph of Section I, in which Hume tells how the inquiry is going to be carried out. He says he expects to discover the true origin of morals by analyzing "personal merit," which he takes to consist of a "complication of mental qualities," that is, of "attributes of the mind" which are estimable or blamable. He considers this to be an easy task—easy in the sense that there could be little difficulty in determining whether any given mental quality is estimable or blamable. All the inquirer has to do, says Hume, is to ask himself whether he would like to have this quality or that ascribed to him. The reader at this point might wonder why Hume is so confident that all persons would agree if they were asked this question about each "mental quality." It is clear that Hume thinks they would, and in reading the ensuing pages the reader should put Hume to the test, to see whether his answers about each quality would indeed be agreed to by all inquirers.

In this paragraph Hume distinguishes two aspects of the inquiry's method: first, "collecting and arranging the estimable or blamable qualities," which can be carried out "without any reasoning"; second, the part of the method that does involve reasoning—the discovery of "the circumstances on both sides which are common to these qualities." From these common circumstances he expects to be able to find "these universal principles from which all censure and approbation is ultimately derived." We see that this discovery would be the solution of the problem to which the inquiry is devoted. And Hume adds that it concerns a "question of fact, not of abstract science," so that we are engaged in an experimental inquiry based on a comparison of particular instances.

The questions we should try to answer in our reading are easy to determine from what this paragraph tells us. And the answers to these questions should give us our first summary statement of the book as a whole. We should find out how the estimable and blamable qualities are "collected and arranged"; what common circumstances Hume finds in the arrangement; and how these circumstances lead us to "the foundation of ethics."

If the reader will make use of the table of contents he will not find it very difficult to formulate, after his first reading, such a summary statement. One might begin as follows:

> The mental qualities are collected and arranged according to a scheme that can be seen to be exhaustive: qualities useful to ourselves or to others, and qualities immediately agreeable to ourselves or to others.

The reader should keep in mind Hume's intention to "consider *every* attribute of the mind which renders a man an object either of esteem and affection or of hatred and contempt" and should ask whether this scheme insures that every such attribute will come under consideration. In answering this question he will see that two exhaustive distinctions are employed, the distinction between the self and the other, and the distinction between what is useful and what is immediately agreeable.[10] It should be noted that only the estimable qualities are arranged; the blamable are evidently considered by Hume to be simply the contraries of these. Then we can see that he considers every estimable quality of mind to be either useful to someone or immediately agreeable to someone. Implicitly, no other possibility is admitted. There is no difficulty about accepting the exhaustiveness of the second distinction: if qualities are useful or agreeable to persons, they must either be so to the persons who possess the qualities, or to other persons—there is no other possibility.

---

[10] An exhaustive distinction is one whose terms, taken together, exhaust all the instances to which that category of terms could possibly apply. The reader of philosophy will find the concept of exhaustive distinction continually important. The simplest example involves negation. We may say, with respect to some given property, that absolutely everything either has that property or it does not. Take, for example, the property of life; we may say of everything that it either has life or not—in saying so we apply an exhaustive distinction, because we take it to exhaust all the possibilities. Philosophers have raised difficulties about the use of this concept; the difficulties can be seen if we alter the example a little and suppose that the distinction between life and death is exhaustive—it is not so clear that absolutely everything is either living or dead. But, although it may be hard in a given case to know whether we are working with an exhaustive distinction, the concept of exhaustive distinction should be clear.

If, in seeking to complete our summary statement, we look back to Hume's indications of what he intended to do (in the penultimate paragraph of Section I), we might try to make the statement reflect three suggestions found there: (1) "collecting and arranging the estimable and blamable qualities of men," (2) "to discover the circumstances on both sides which are common to these qualities," (3) "and thence to reach the foundation of ethics and find those universal principles from which all censure or approbation is ultimately derived." But the inquiry does not take these steps one after the other; they are closely bound up together. In particular, "common circumstances" are already involved in the scheme according to which we have indicated that "arrangement" of qualities. The qualities in each group share the circumstance that makes the group a group (e.g., the social virtues share the circumstance of being useful to others). If we try to take account of this point, and add a reference to the foundation of ethics, our complete statement may run as follows:

> The inquiry collects and arranges the estimable qualities of men in four groups: qualities useful to others, useful to ourselves, immediately agreeable to ourselves, and immediately agreeable to others. Rational consideration of the four groups leads to the conclusion that the foundation of ethics is the class of benevolent sentiments, from which all approbation is ultimately derived.[11]

We may now use this statement as a point of departure for approaching Hume's text. The procedure will be similar to that em-

---

11 This statement does take account of the first two steps enumerated immediately above, and the reference to "the foundation of ethics" in the third. The "universal principles" that are referred to may seem to be ignored. There is room for difference of interpretation here, but I believe that the difficulty results from our limiting our analysis to the nine sections of the *Inquiry*, whose central concern is the foundation of ethics. There is *one* foundation and there are *many* principles, as is indicated by the title of the book, and by such expressions as "universal principles" and "general principles." The many principles require, for their full treatment, the appendixes as well as the nine sections. Notice, in this connection, the first sentence of Appendix I: "If the foregoing hypothesis be received, it will now be easy for us to determine the question first started, concerning the general principles of morals. . . ."

ployed in the treatment of *Macbeth*: we shall ask how some of the details of the text fit this summary statement.[12]

A number of questions arise very naturally. Two main lines of questioning, closely interrelated, may be mentioned. First, how are the main parts of the text accounted for by our initial summary statement? Second, can the order of these parts, and the emphases that result from it, be well accounted for? Also, it would be only natural, now that we are engaged in a second reading, to keep in mind the two controversies that received so much attention in Section I (about the reality of moral distinctions, and about reason and sentiment). One more distinction that should be in the reader's mind in a second reading is the distinction between "the speculative" and "the practical part of morals," mentioned early in Section II[13] and prominent in Part II of Section IX.

The first part of our summary statement goes far toward accounting for the presence of the main parts of the text. The first sentence of the conclusion (Section IX) has told us that "*personal merit* consists altogether in the possession of mental qualities, *useful* or *agreeable* to the *person himself* or to *others*."[14] Sections II, III, VI, VII, and VIII are devoted to these four kinds of "virtue" (as Hume sometimes refers to the mental qualities); and Part I of Section IX is concerned with drawing conclusions from examining them. What then, it is natural to ask, is the function of Sections IV and V, and of Part II of Section IX?

---

[12] An essay such as this one might usefully be much longer. Its greater length could result from the same sort of testing of a number of different summary statements, taken as alternative starting points for reflective interpretation. Some of these could certainly lead to blind alleys—the reader would conclude, after he had tested them for a while against some of the details of the text, that they simply would not do and would have to be abandoned. Such experiences should be expected in philosophical reading. I have tried, however, to select provisional interpretations that lead to modification and elaboration, rather than to abandonment.

[13] P. 10.

[14] We may note that Hume goes on here to offer a proof of the exhaustiveness of his arrangement that is different from those suggested above (n. 10). He does not show that there are no other *possibilities*. Instead, he says that if anyone were to impute all four qualities to a given person ("Cleanthes") that person would be "a model of perfect virtue" (p. 91).

When we ask why Sections IV and V are in the book, we are led at once to a question of order, because these two sections seem, at first glance, to interrupt an orderly progression from "Qualities Useful to Others" to the remaining three kinds of qualities. As we reflect on this matter we will notice that the first two qualities considered (in Sections II, III, and VI) are *useful,* and the second two (discussed in Sections VII and VIII) are *immediately agreeable.* We see, then, that Hume wishes first to emphasize the useful qualities, those which share the circumstance of utility; so Sections IV and V fall readily into place, because both are concerned with utility. From Section I through Section VI the reader can find many ways in which utility is stressed. Section IV might even be regarded as a digression (since it does not treat a mental quality), except for the fact that political society is said to owe its very existence to utility. Only part of the merit of benevolence is due to its utility (and the other part, ultimately, is even more important, for Hume's moral theory); yet it is the utility of benevolence that Hume wishes to stress first.

Questions about the function of Sections IV and V have involved us in questions about the order of the various sections. It will be illuminating to continue with this line of questioning, even though we might turn (as our summary statement could have led us to do) to another question, about Part II of Section IX (since the statement does not readily account for that part).[15]

Continuing then with the question of the order in which Hume takes up his various topics, let us first ask why benevolence should be the first of the mental qualities examined. It is perfectly natural that it should be, for it seems to him to be the most obviously estimable of the mental qualities; this is the burden of his first observations about it.[16] It is less natural that he should treat benevolence

---

[15] The reader should not be too rigid in holding to a provisional plan of attack. Certain lines of analysis may arise before the provisional plan has been carried out, and if they seem promising there is no reason why the analysis should not turn to them. It is hard to formulate any hard and fast rules to guide the reader in his choice of questions to consider.

[16] Hume is not alone in this opinion. Later in the eighteenth century Kant began the first section of his *Fundamental Principles of the Metaphysics of Morals* with the famous sentence: "Nothing can possibly be conceived in the

first as utilitarian (it has already appeared that his decision to do this is calculated, rather than "natural"). Nevertheless it is reasonable that he should do so. We readily grant that from the point of view of the *spectator* (a term we shall find to be very important later on), which can be distinguished from the point of view of one who possesses the virtue, what is chiefly in mind when benevolence is praised is its beneficial character—its usefulness. To call attention to this circumstance, as Hume does in the first sentence of Part II of Section II, is clearly in accord with the method described at the end of Section I.

How are other aspects of the book's structure affected by Hume's decision to begin by considering the utility of benevolence? He calls benevolence and justice *social virtues*. The term *social* indicates that these virtues are useful to society, that is, to persons other than the person (the self) who possesses the virtues. So Hume has in mind from the outset not merely the useful-agreeable (qualities agreeable to others are treated later, in Section VIII) but also the self-other distinction. Justice, like benevolence, is a virtue that has had great importance in ethical theory (Plato's *Republic* centers upon it). Here there is an easy progression from benevolence, part of whose merit lies in its utility, to justice, whose sole origin is its public utility; the same progression leads easily to political society, as has been noted

The manner in which Section II begins the discussion of benevolence not only leads smoothly into the immediately succeeding topics. Hume is ingenious in suggesting matters in Section II that will have to be discussed later. For one thing, he finds benevolence so estimable that he cannot keep from giving the impression, as he describes its estimability, that he is "recommending generosity and benevolence." This gives him an occasion for saying that his object

world, or even out of it, which can be called good without qualification, except a *good will*" (Abbott translation). Kant's moral theory is significantly different from Hume's, which should warn us that his "good will" may not be quite the same as Hume's "benevolence"; yet the two words are similar in meaning, and it is impressive that each philosopher gives his term so preeminent a position among good things.

is "more the speculative than the practical part of morals." This in itself is an important indication of the nature of the book as Hume intends it; it also anticipates the discussion in Part II of Section IX. Second, he carefully qualifies the stress he gives to the usefulness of benevolence by saying expressly that the merit of benevolence arises *in part* from its beneficial tendencies, and he promises to consider later "how considerable a part" that is.[17]

Our reflections have brought out some things that are emphasized in the early stages in ways that are not indicated by our summary statement. Let us now consider the early stages in a little greater detail. Taking note of the fact that Sections II and III are each divided into two parts, we may ask whether the two parts function in the same way in both sections. The intentions of the two sections are so clearly different, however, that we see this is not the case. The two parts of Section II follow the method set forth in Section I. We consider first whether benevolence is estimable, and we find no problem in saying that it is. The only problem seems to be the next one, of observing the circumstance common to all benevolent qualities,[18] and that problem is given to Part II, which tells us that at least part of its merit derives from its usefulness. In Section III, on the other hand, the problem is not to prove that at least part of the merit of justice is due to its usefulness; it is rather to prove that usefulness is the sole foundation of its merit —even of its existence. If we go through the four parts of Sections II and III one after the other, we find that it is the second (Part II of Section II) that first gives stress to utility, that Part I of Section III stresses it more strongly, and Part II of Section III still more strongly. In Part II of Section III Hume finds that justice cannot be established by reasoning alone; that knowledge of human nature must also be taken into account; and that even that general knowledge is not enough; for, although all men share the same nature,

---

[17] P. 14.

[18] It should be noted that in the case of benevolence we are dealing with a whole family of qualities, many of which are indicated in the second sentence of Section II. One of these, humanity, comes more and more to be regarded as synonymous with benevolence (sympathy also attains a similar status).

their lives are varied by different circumstances, and these have to be taken into account in civil laws. The establishment of justice becomes more perfect as men move from the universal laws of reason, through the less universal laws of human nature, to the particular circumstances·in which men actually live. At each step in the perfection of justice utility is the principle that determines the laws.

The increasing importance that utility takes on as the inquiry progresses is also shown in Section IV, "Of Political Society." Justice will not materialize unless men take human nature and particular circumstances into account. And it will not materialize outside of political society. Each condition required for the establishment of justice is useful because it helps bring justice about, and we would have no need for justice except for its utility. Furthermore, it is utility that tells men precisely how, in their search for justice, they should determine their laws and construct their political societies.

We should not leave our initial reflections on Sections II and III without asking just what benevolence and justice are, for Hume; and we can get some light on this by comparing the two sections. What do our basic distinctions suggest? The self-other distinction suggests that benevolence is unselfish, and that—at least in comparison—justice is selfish. This is worth noting, even if it be taken now in only a provisional way. The useful-agreeable distinction suggests that justice is closer to the useful, and benevolence to the agreeable. We are not truly benevolent if we act in the expectation of getting something in return. Justice, on the other hand, is for Hume based on the idea that we respect the property of others because they agree to respect ours.

The contrast between benevolence and justice can be explored in two ways. First, it is apparent that the term *property* is central to Hume's conception of justice, and that justice is an affair that makes no sense except between persons who are in important respects equals. In contrast, benevolence is possible in cases where justice is not; notably, it is possible between persons who are not equal (where justice could make no sense). If benevolence were universal, it would not be necessary even for equals to agree to respect one another's property; there would be no need for justice. Second (and this point is more useful for our purposes as reflective readers, because it casts more light on many later passages of the book), the unselfish-selfish contrast between benevolence and justice bears strongly upon Hume's great interest in what he calls "self-love," and the theories that take it to be the principle of morality.

In Section II, even though benevolence is considered with reference to utility—to its satisfaction of somebody's interest—it is not entitled "to the general good will and approbation of mankind" because it serves the interests of the benevolent person himself, but because it "proceeds from a tender sympathy with *others*."[19] Nor is it estimable because it serves the interests of those who are doing the praising. When a man is praised because he benefits his parents, children, friends, domestics, and others, who is praising him? Not the parents, children, friends, and domestics, but some other disinterested party. In contrast justice, although it too is considered a quality useful to others, is not even possible unless it tends to benefit the just man as well as those to whom he is just. Thus justice is essentially selfish, even though, like benevolence, it can be praised for its "public utility."

The points that have just been made can be found in the text if it is approached with the useful-agreeable and the self-other distinctions in mind. There is one other important point which can be found in the text, although the distinction it involves has not yet been brought out. That is that benevolence is a *natural* quality, whereas justice is not; the same point could be differently expressed by saying that benevolence is an *original* quality, whereas justice is *derivative*. The point, and its bearing upon the selfish and unselfish characteristics of justice and benevolence, respectively, can be seen where Hume says that if external conveniences were sufficiently abundant "every other social virtue would flourish and receive tenfold increase; but the cautious, jealous virtue of justice would never once have been dreamed of."[20] Later, especially in

---

[19] P. 10; my italics.
[20] P. 15.

Appendix II, Hume argues that the so-called selfish passions are no more natural than the unselfish. Here in Sections II and III he seems to go further and to consider benevolence, which is unselfish, to be natural; justice, which is founded upon private interest, would not exist at all, if only human nature were involved.

The connections between the two distinctions, self-other and original-derivative, and their bearing upon benevolence and justice can help the reader see why the self-love theory of morals looms so large in Hume's thoughts. If there is one main controversy that he is engaged in, it is with those who support the "selfish hypothesis." These theorists hold that there is no natural passion which is not selfish. Hume's attack on the selfish hypothesis requires the use of the original-derivative distinction. It enables him to reach his conclusion in Section IX, and by means of that conclusion to develop other ideas in Appendixes I, II, and III (some which were anticipated in Section I, but regarded there as impossible to clear up before the true origin of morals had been discovered).

According to the interpretation that this essay is developing, Hume deliberately anticipates his ultimate conclusion in his presentation of these two most estimable virtues, benevolence and justice. He wants the reader to continue to keep in mind the question about the true origin of morals, and the question in his mind could be expressed by a modification of the question Hume asks in Section V: Is the foundation of morals "self-interest," or some "more generous motive"?[21]

The two lines of questioning mentioned above about the extent to which our summary statement accounts for the main parts of the text and about the order of those parts, have brought our analysis to a question raised in Section V: Why does utility please? The question that concluded our last paragraph is the very question Section V deals with. So we can see why Section V is in the book (first line of questioning) and why it occurs where it does (second line). A few more observations about its connections with other sections may be pertinent, before we turn to details of Section V itself.

---

[21] P. 43.

Section V is the very center of the nine sections, and may well be expected to present a turning point in the inquiry. Its concern for a question about utility follows naturally after the utilitarian concerns of Sections II through IV; but its question, Why does utility please? is significantly new. Its central location and its connection with the utilitarian concerns of the preceding sections suggests that it may also have some significant connection with the non-utilitarian concerns of the succeeding sections. We must note, however, that the structure is not neatly symmetrical, since the immediately succeeding Section VI is utilitarian, "Of Qualities Useful to Ourselves." In noting this fact our attention may be called to another, namely, that Section V follows the treatment of the social virtues and precedes the treatment of what might be called "private virtues." We might think that Section V completes the discussion of the social virtues, but it turns out that the subject matter of Section VIII is more social than private. We shall return to this difficulty later. But now, as we turn to a detailed consideration of Section V let us keep in mind that it may be making a transition from concern for "public utility" to "private" merit, and—although less clearly—a transition from the useful to the agreeable. (The later transition is less clearly taking place, because Section VI is still concerned with the useful. The difficulty may, however, suggest to us that, even though it is ostensibly concerned with utility, Section VI may in fact be oriented toward the agreeable, precisely because of what is said in Section V.)

What is the meaning of the title of Section V, "Why Utility Pleases"? What does the term *utility* mean for Hume? In the table of contents its synonym, *usefulness*, stands in contrast to what is immediately agreeable. This suggests that utility can be at best mediately agreeable, that it pleases as a means to some end, some end immediately pleasant. This makes sense, and much of the detail of Section V does treat utility as a means toward some desired end (he speaks of the public utility of virtues which have a tendency to promote some end that is in some way agreeable to us). But if there is some end that pleases us immediately, of course the means to that end may please us *mediately*. If Hume meant no more than this he would be making a point that hardly needs a section to explain it. But it would not be trivial if the title meant, "Why Utility Is Immediately Agreeable." The distinctions we have been working with seem to offer no possible meanings for the title except this one, and the other that appears trivial.

Our approach to the analysis of Section V has placed the self-love issue in relief; and it is clearly the most important issue discussed in the section. Within the section the issue arises from the very natural thought that those virtues that are esteemed because of their "public utility" tend to produce ends (i.e., are means to ends) that "must be in some way agreeable to us and take hold of some natural affection."[21] The reader is being asked to think in terms of means and ends, a distinction which is parallel to the useful-agreeable distinction. The terms *agreeable* and *natural affection* demand reflection, in connection with each other. Hume is using them in order to bring out a connection between the ends that are immediately agreeable to us, on the one hand, and human nature, on the other. The term *nature* has special importance at this point. Hume has just concluded that it is nature rather than education which is at the foundation of moral distinctions,[22] and the first footnote to Part II of Section V is especially illuminating as an indication of what Hume is seeking as the origin of morals. What is natural must be contrasted with something in some sense not natural. What is agreeable and takes hold of a natural affection is immediately pleasant; such are the ends which useful things have a tendency to promote. The means themselves (and they have the utility that this section is concerned with) stand in contrast, and it is therefore reasonable to regard them as in a sense unnatural, and mediately pleasant. It should not be considered derogatory to call them unnatural—they are not wrong, or perverted. They are simply utilized deliberately—with thought, instead of naturally, or automatically.

After he has established the natural attractiveness of the ends

[21] P. 43.

[22] Recall the original pretense that the controversy about the reality of moral distinctions is not worth considering.

that useful qualities tend to promote, Hume turns to the question, What is the natural affection that agreeable ends take hold of? He answers first with an exhaustive distinction: "It must please either from considerations of self-interest or from more generous motives." The next task must be to determine which of these alternatives is the source of the pleasure.

How would the reader now be expected to answer this question? The self-love controversy is very much on Hume's mind, and he assumes that on a first reading—before reflection—the reader may answer, "It must please for considerations of self-interest." Hume believes that his own contrary answer can be established only after the self-love issue has been clarified, and that is why he turns to it in Part II of Section V. Why is it so much in need of clarification at this point? Consider together two things Hume has done thus far: first, he has put great stress on utility, and, second, he has made use of the self-other distinction, although it greatly needs to be made more precise. We are engaged in our second reading, so we know that Hume ultimately denies the basic character of the selfish-unselfish distinction, at least with reference to the passions.[23] As reflective readers we should realize that this denial must be made to harmonize with the use, throughout Sections II–VII, of the self-other distinction. As we reflect on this problem it may also occur to us that the self-love controversy is closely related to it. If, then, the self-other distinction must be refined, in order to prevent the reader from misinterpreting the stress placed on utility, is this refinement not exactly what Hume has in mind in Part II of Section V, where the subject is self-love?

Before proceeding, the reader ought to realize that Hume's facility in writing often gives a specious appearance of simplicity. Here we have an instance of considerable complexity. We must keep not only the self-other distinction in mind but also two others: the one between the useful and the agreeable (which is also bound up with the mediate-immediate distinction), and the one between what is original and what is derivative.

After having stated the exhaustive distinction between self-

---

[23] Pp. 92–94.

interest and more generous motives, what does Hume do in the remaining paragraphs of Part I of Section V? He considers whether it would be reasonable to explain all interests or motives in terms of self-interest. His negative answer is given in the final paragraph of Part I. It follows a passage in which he argues, first, that we often praise useful actions which actually do not affect our interests, and, second, that our praise cannot be explained by saying that we imagine our interests to be affected. The final paragraph (which should be read very carefully) points out that the useful actions we approve of are indeed "for somebody's interest," but not necessarily "our own only." We are, therefore, "not totally indifferent" to interests other than our own. But how are we related to such interests? Hume would say, as *spectators*. He has made some reference to the "spectator" or "beholder" in previous pages, but scarcely enough to indicate how important the idea is. It is the relevance to morals of our reactions as spectators that Hume means by the term *principle*, in the final sentence of Part I of Section V: "By opening up this principle we shall discover one great source of moral distinctions." Let us see then how he opens it up.

Hume begins Part II of Section V by explaining that it is in the interest of simplicity and "unity of principle" that other philosophers reduce all our praising and blaming to self-interest. He then re-emphasizes that we have seen (in Part I) instances where private interest did not enter in at all, and yet we praised or blamed. To this re-emphasis on the conclusion of Part I he appends the first footnote to Part II, which has already been referred to. What is the force of this footnote? What are the important terms it employs? *Humanity, principle, human nature. Principle* seems especially important, and it is qualified in certain ways. Principles are considered according to degrees of generality, simplicity, universality, and originality. In making his point here how does he apply these terms? Humanity (or fellow-feeling, or benevolence) is a principle of human nature. As such it is original, that is, it is not derived from ("deduced from") any more general principle—it is "taken hold of" immediately (not by means of some chain linking it actually or in imagination to self-interest). If it is not really original ("if it were possible . . . [to] resolve it into principles more simple and universal") it is to be taken in this *Inquiry* as original. Although it may be possible to resolve it into others more simple and general, these others are not meant, by Hume, to include the principle of self-love. He is insisting that humanity, fellow-feeling, benevolence are original, in the sense that they are not derived from any passions supposedly more basic, such as the so-called "selfish passions."

In "opening up this principle" Hume proceeds to consider "the force of humanity and benevolence." Two kinds of questions can guide such a consideration: (1) What is the range or scope of this sort of feeling? To what kinds of things does it respond? And such questions also ask, implicitly, Does it respond to all the actions with which morality is concerned? (2) How strong is this sort of feeling? Is it strong enough to move men to moral action? And these questions also ask, implicitly, If they are or can be strong enough to move men to action, do they move men "naturally" to moral rather than to immoral action? and, if not, can they be made to move them to moral action, and, if so, how? We shall find that all these questions are faced in Part II of Section V.

Hume's answer to the first question is that the moral range of the principle is unlimited: " . . . no passion, when well represented, can be utterly indifferent to us, because there is none of which every man has not within him at least the seeds and first principles."[24] How does he hope to get his reader to see this? The paragraphs that lead up to this statement develop the idea previously referred to, the idea of the spectator. Two points are dwelt on. (1) We are all spectators of life. We are interested in the events that we see happen, even if they do not serve our own selfish interests. (2) Poetry and the poets, and historians too, exploit our interest in such events. In fact, it could be said that much history, and even more poetry, presents matters that do not immediately engage the welfare of the reader. Toward them we take the attitude of a spectator. What do history and poetry show us that is helpful to our

---

[24] P. 50.

inquiry? They provide answers to the first sort of question by showing the great range of things that readers of history and poetry are interested in; it includes or can include everything of possible moral importance. And they show us something about the strength of these interests, and here we have answers to the second sort of question. Different historical and poetic subjects arouse weaker or stronger feelings, and the strength of the feelings may also depend on the skill of the historian or poet. Here we have an indication of an answer to the implied question, How can these feelings be made to move men to moral rather than immoral action? The indication is scanty here and is more fully developed later, but it consists in showing that these feelings can be affected by what is said by skillful users of words. It is also implied that men are not simply good or bad by nature; they have natural capacities which can be cultivated so as to make them good.

With reference to the second sort of question, about the strength of the feelings we have as spectators, Hume is careful to point out that "the passions excited may not always be so strong and steady as to have great influence on the conduct and behavior."[25] Toward the end of his consideration of the range and strength of our spectator feelings Hume mentions briefly (and treats more fully in the conclusion) two forces that can control and develop these natural feelings: judgment and social intercourse. "Judgment here corrects the inequalities of our internal connections and perceptions," and "the intercourse of sentiments . . . in society and conversation makes us form some general unalterable standard by which we may approve or disapprove of characters and manners."[26]

When Hume says, five paragraphs from the end of Section V, "Thus, in whatever light we take this subject," it may look as though he is merely summing up the conclusions he has reached. He is summing up, but do not the final paragraphs give new significance to these conclusions? Note that Hume's retrospective glance,

[25] P. 50.
[26] Pp. 55–56.

in "Thus . . . this subject," takes in not only Section V but the preceding sections too, since he applies the conclusions to the social virtues. What are we now able to say about them? That the natural sentiment of benevolence is the chief source of the merit attributed to them. This helps us see why the inquiry began with benevolence rather than justice. It also shows us that justice, although in itself a "cautious, jealous virtue," is approved of not merely because it tends to serve the interest of those who approve of it but also, and primarily, because it has great utility for society as a whole, and we all naturally approve of such utility, independently of the fact that it may serve our own interests. The ideas were not presented in this way in Sections II, III, and IV.

In the same place (five paragraphs from the end) Hume points out that we now have "the faint rudiments at least, or outlines, of a general distinction between actions." It is easy to see that this remark is reminiscent of the very first paragraphs of the book, where the controversy about the reality of moral distinctions was mentioned and then discarded as a subject to be considered. The reader may naturally ask why Hume seems to resolve the controversy after all. The remark is related to that controversy, but does it really resolve it? Surely not, as the controversy was originally presented. Hume has supposed from the beginning that his readers do not doubt the reality of moral distinctions. But he does think they would have learned, by the end of Section V, that there is one "general distinction." It is a distinction between the feelings we have about what promotes the happiness of our fellow creatures and those we have about what tends to bring about their misery. He thinks they would have learned that these feelings can acquire vigor in proportion to the humanity of the persons who feel them, their connection with those who are benefited or injured, and their lively conception of their happiness or misery. We have then not only an outline of a general distinction, but an outline of a moral theory in this paragraph. For, as the following sentences show, our sympathies, though originally weak, are capable of being enlivened (this is implicit in the terms just used: *humanity, connection, lively conception*). It is implied here, in connection with the previous observation that passions are not always strong enough to influence our conduct, that by enlivening our sympathies for our fellow creatures we become more moral in our actions (and this implication is made explicit in the conclusion, Section IX).

If we look ahead now to Sections VI, VII, and VIII, we are reminded, by the fact that they deal in turn with three of the four kinds of mental qualities, that through Section V we have been concerned with only one of these kinds, qualities useful to others. If we revert to the point made at the end of Part I of Section V, we may express that point in different words. There it was said that we are not totally indifferent to interests which are not our own. Let us now say that such interests are immediately agreeable to us. If we are not indifferent to them, and if they do not serve our own interest (i.e., if they are not useful to us), they must be immediately agreeable. Then, although the social virtues were first presented as useful to others, it is possible and important to consider them as immediately agreeable to anyone who views them as a spectator. Perhaps all the mental qualities can be considered as immediately agreeable. The reader should go through the remaining sections of the book carefully, with this idea in mind. This discussion will have to do so quickly, calling attention to only a few points.

Section V finishes by saying that "the progress of the argument will bring a further confirmation of the present theory."[27] How does Section VI, "Of Qualities Useful to Ourselves," confirm it? First, does it not bear nicely on the self-love controversy? The self-love theorist can make his case best with reference to the "public and social virtues," because everyone seems to profit from these. In this section, however, we are considering what Hume calls "the private or selfish virtues," virtues useful to the person who

---

[27] Here and in the passage referred to in note 28, where Hume says we "cannot . . . hesitate any longer," it is apparent that he considers the theory to have been developed. The primarily "confirmatory" character of Sections VII and VIII is indicated by the fact that they are not, like the others, divided into two parts, and are brief.

possesses them. It follows, Hume argues, that if we can approve these selfish qualities when they are not useful to us, we "cannot consistently hesitate any longer with regard to disinterested benevolence, patriotism, and humanity."[28]

Probably the most important confirmation provided by Section VII has already been referred to: it is connected with the appearance of benevolence, the first of the virtues to be treated as a social virtue, under the heading of qualities agreeable to ourselves. It is at the very least striking that Hume should consider benevolence a "selfish virtue." We may recall that the earlier treatment of benevolence found that a "*considerable* part of that esteem which is universally paid to it,"[29] arises from its utility. Here Hume tells us of another source of that esteem. This is an important point and should not be misunderstood. The other part of its esteem is really different from utility; it is not something indirectly traceable to it. Benevolence itself, as a possession of the benevolent person (for whom it is not useful), is immediately agreeable.

It was said above (p. 115) that we would return later to a difficulty presented by Section VIII, that is, by its being concerned with qualities agreeable to others, after the concern seemed to have shifted, in Sections V through VII, to ourselves. The reason for reverting to others can be traced to the fact that the force of benevolence can be felt in every area of morals. Benevolence was introduced as a quality useful to others; but it is also useful and agreeable to ourselves, and now—in Section VIII—agreeable to others. Those of its features that have been disclosed in Sections VI and VII help us to see another feature that Hume considers remarkable, and that is the extent to which feelings of benevolence communicate themselves to the spectator. By taking special note of this Hume prepares for the special importance that the term *sympathy* has in the conclusion (Section IX). It is this quality of sympathy, which is either the same thing as benevolence and humanity or benevolence and humanity considered in a certain way, that gives

[28] P. 67.
[29] P. 80.

this principle its greatest potentiality for the development of morals.[30]

Other confirmations of the present theory can be found in Section VIII. At the outset, in the footnote that Hume appends to its title, the reader can find confirmation of the importance of the spectator idea. In the definition of virtue given in this footnote, as "a quality of the mind agreeable to or approved of by everyone who considers or contemplates it," the expression "everyone who considers or contemplates" must mean the same thing as "spectator." The rest of the note is also interesting, because it singles out "the class of virtues here considered" (qualities immediately agreeable to others) as qualities that produce pleasure "more immediately" than any of the others. If we can see why they do so, we can gain an important confirmation of the theory.

We must take the spectator idea very seriously if we are to understand this point. It is the approval or disapproval that others give, disinterested others, that is the foundation of morals. The disinterested spectator gets immediate pleasure from qualities useful to others (interested others)—from contemplating those qualities. His pleasure, however, is not absolutely immediate, because it seems to depend upon the thought that the others whose interests are served by those qualities are accordingly pleased. The situation is similar with respect to qualities useful to ourselves, generally speaking. Benevolence is an exception, because it is not only immediately agreeable to the spectator who is pleased by the spectacle of a benevolent person (and—as has just been said—this is distinct from being pleased by the utility of benevolence); it is also agreeable to the spectator because the pleasure of being benevolent communicates itself to the spectator "by a contagion of natural sympathy."[31] Here the spectator does not have to *think* of the

---

[30] This point is most fully developed in Part II of Section IX.

[31] I "borrow" this phrase from Section VII (p. 74), but it seems fair to apply it to benevolence, considered as a quality immediately agreeable to others. The note under discussion, although appended to Section VIII, can be understood as an application to "others" of what is said about ourselves in Section VII.

pleasure felt by or given by the benevolent man. The pleasure in all three cases (the benevolent man, the person he benefits, and the disinterested spectator) has very much the same quality.

After discussing a list of qualities immediately agreeable to others, Hume finishes with one he describes as "a *manner*, a grace, an ease, a genteelness, and I-know-not-what" which "catches our affection . . . suddenly and powerfully" but which he presents as inexplicable, "a part of ethics left by nature to baffle all the pride of philosophy."[32] But does he mean that it fails to confirm his theory? Surely not. Precisely because it pleases so immediately, not by virtue of anything else that can be pointed to in explanation, it fits and confirms the theory, whether or not an explanation can be found—or perhaps precisely because one is impossible.

We will not give detailed attention to Section IX, the conclusion, but the reader must not misunderstand the reasons for this. I hope that the treatment of the first eight sections contains a sufficient number of suggestions that can guide the reader in his approach to many works of philosophy. I do not mean that a grasp of what has been done so far will make a full understanding of the conclusion easy—far from it. The reasoning in this final section is intricate, more so than may be apparent to most readers on first acquaintance. But it is recommended that the reader attempt now to find significance in the conclusion which escaped him on his first rapid reading but which comes to light now that the rest of the book has been more carefully analyzed. I add only a few suggestions to guide him in this task.

If the reader will make an outline of this final section he will find that Hume begins with a sort of summary of a "proof" that personal merit consists of the four kinds of quality that have been studied. He reaffirms that "there is some benevolence, however small, infused into our bosom."[33] In stressing the "however small" he again turns to the self-love theory, and becomes involved in a comparison of benevolence with passions "vulgarly, though im-

---

[32] P. 89.

[33] The quotations in this paragraph can be found between pages 92 and 94.

properly . . . . denominated selfish."[33] The remainder of Part I of Section IX does not merely confirm "the present theory." It faces new questions too. If we say that benevolence is a natural feeling, one felt by all men, are there not other natural feelings, and if so, why are they not principles of morals? Moreover, since it is clear that there are other natural feelings, notably the so-called selfish ones, are they not also stronger—at least in some men, and probably in most—than the feeling of benevolence? The reader should notice, in seeking Hume's solution of this difficulty, that there is a difference between recognizing what morals are and forming general ideas of human conduct, on the one hand, and developing moral character and behavior, on the other; there is a difference, and the former have an effect upon the latter. This fact gives rise to another question dealt with in this part: How do our general ideas about morality tend to make men moral?

In Section II Hume has said that the object of his *Inquiry* is "more the speculative than the practical part of morals," but in Part II of Section IX he does turn to the latter. To inquire into the practical part of morals amounts to asking how a mere spectator (who, after all, *speculates*) can become one who acts, and acts morally. But the text concerns itself more expressly with the selfish-unselfish distinction and asks whether it is in our self-interest to act, as it were, disinterestedly; for, in becoming moral do we not learn to respect the interests of others? It turns out, since the "selfish" passions are improperly so-called, that nothing "is more fit [to be a basis to self-love] than benevolence or humanity."[34] If at this point the reader can view the four classes of virtues as general ideas formulated by our speculative inquiry, he can see that the last use Hume makes of them is to show how these ideas, when understood (and in understanding them reason plays its supporting role in the development of morals), are naturally attractive when put into practice, so that a true speculative inquiry into the principles of morals "may contribute to the amendment of men's lives."[35]

---

[34] P. 101.

[35] P. 99.

II

From the study of Hume's *Inquiry concerning the Principles of Morals* we cannot learn rules or procedures that can be followed rigidly in approaching *any* book in philosophy. Each work must be approached in terms peculiarly appropriate to it. Nevertheless, what we have seen in Hume may be generally suggestive, and should at least be useful in a negative way, when we turn to other works. We may, as we turn to them, try first to see how they respond to us if we come to them with questions or attitudes like those we have developed for Hume's book. We would not have to go very far before finding that other works are very different, in many ways. Without going into the same detail in the examination we shall take fragments of two other works, works deliberately chosen because of significant differences from Hume's *Inquiry*, in spite of their similarity in subject matter—they all deal with something we may call *virtue*. The two works are Plato's dialogue *Meno* and John Dewey's *Human Nature and Conduct*.[36]

We shall arbitrarily limit our attention to about the first half of the *Meno*, up to page 86d of the Stephanus edition.[37] Although this gives us only a fragment, we shall assume that the fragment constitutes a unity of a significant sort. Therefore it will be feasible and desirable to try to summarize this fragment, as we tried to summarize Hume's *Inquiry*. We shall begin, then, with the same introductory tasks: the determination of the chief problem of the

---

[36] Many translations of the *Meno* are available. The reader of this essay must have one at hand. An inexpensive edition of the Jowett translation is published in the Library of Liberal Arts (1949). The complete text of *Human Nature and Conduct* is in the Modern Library (1930), but its first section, which we shall discuss, is included as a supplement to the present volume.

[37] Page references will be to the standard Stephanus edition. Most editions in English include, in addition to their own pagination, some indications of points that correspond to points in the Stephanus edition. The Stephanus pages are subdivided by the first five letters of the alphabet, so that page 86d, for example, is on the lower half of page 86.

work, and of the conclusion that is reached, and the formulation of a summary statement indicating the problem, the conclusion, and—as concisely as possible—how the conclusion, is reached.

The *Meno*, unlike Hume's *Inquiry*, tells us nothing by its title, unless we happen to know something about the historical person Meno (who is not a fictitious character); nor does it have a table of contents. The opening pages, however, like those of Hume, expressly reflect on what the problem of the discussion should be. It is, nevertheless, probably more difficult—at least with the fragment we are considering—to determine what the problem really is, because it keeps changing. It is, first, How does one acquire virtue? It becomes, What is virtue? It then becomes, How can we define anything? And, after an answer to that problem is presented, Meno reinstates the original problem, How is virtue acquired? And this problem remains central for the rest of the dialogue (although in this discussion we are not concerned with the last part).

It is hard to arrive at the sort of statement we seek, unless we can consider the main parts of the work, and how they are interrelated. Although we have no table of contents, we do find in the *Meno*, as in many Platonic dialogues, obvious indications of dividing points between parts. These are most clearly marked when shifts of speaker occur; when, for example, Socrates turns from Meno to his slave boy and, later, back to Meno; again, even when the same two speakers continue to talk, the roles of questioner and answerer are changed, as at 75b, where Meno says, "I would rather that you answer, Socrates," and again at 77b where Meno fulfills his promise to resume the answerer's role. These shifts do divide the dialogue into parts, and the reader should expect these parts to differ in significant ways: they may differ in subject matter, in approach, in the degree to which what is said is reliable, and so on. The reader should be alert to these shifts, but he should also remember that some of them may be in the nature of digressions, or of arguments that merely support more important arguments; and they may also constitute gradual approaches to or arrivals at the main problem, or the conclusion.

When the first reading of the fragment has been completed, an initial summary should be written. It might run as follows:

When Meno asks, How is virtue acquired? Socrates asks, What is virtue? Meno tries unsuccessfully to answer this question, and finally asks how it is possible to learn what *anything* is. Socrates replies that we learn by recollecting and shows how an ignorant slave boy can be led to a geometrical truth merely by being made to answer questions and using only ideas he already has.

This summary is surely very unsatisfactory, and tells us much less about the substance of the dialogue than our summary of Hume's *Inquiry* told us about its substance. Nevertheless it can be useful to us in our reflective reading, if we try to find out, by applying it to the text itself, why it is so unsatisfactory.

Perhaps it should first be recognized that the summary is not without merits. It would be even worse than it is if, in the interests of conciseness (which should always be kept in mind in summing up, because it tends to sharpen one's eye for essentials), we were to leave out proper names, and simply say, in an impersonal way, that it is difficult to define virtue, and that the difficulty directs attention to new problems, such as problems of the theory of knowledge. Such a summary will not do, if we find it important that it is Meno who has difficulty defining virtue, Meno, the very person who has asked how virtue is acquired; and that he has this difficulty in spite of the help Socrates gives him, although an ignorant slave boy is able to profit from Socrates' help and to "recollect" a geometrical theorem he has never heard of. The reader who feels that these matters are important will ask what sort of man Meno is represented to be, how his character affects the meanings of the questions he asks and the nature of the answers he seeks, and what bearing his character has upon the intellectual difficulties he encounters. Because our treatment of the *Meno* here is sketchy, we will not follow up these questions, but any careful reading of the dialogue requires it.

The remainder of the discussion of the *Meno* will focus upon three shortcomings in our summary. First, the reader must feel that very little is said in merely alluding to Meno's inability to define virtue, and in saying that he wonders how it is possible to learn anything. Second, it sounds absurd or even mystical to say only that learning is recollection, especially if we add, as we might, that learning is recollecting things we knew before we were born. Third, the mere statement that an ignorant boy can learn a geometrical theorem by merely answering questions omits the really significant point. We should want to know how it is possible for him to do this, and what it tells us about learning.

The Definition of Virtue

How could we give more significance to our statement that Meno is unable to define virtue? We may first note that his inability is demonstrated by the fact that he tries unsuccessfully several times. We could take each of his efforts, successively, and try to see where he goes wrong in each case. A thorough analysis should of course do this, but we might shorten the procedure if we center our attention on some crucial point and try to find in it some general reason for Meno's failures. Along this line it would be natural to look at his final effort. We can find encouragement for taking this step in the fact that the final effort is highly dramatized by Plato. Meno's frustration leads him to express one of Plato's most famous figures, in which Socrates' effect upon his interlocutors is compared with the paralyzing sting of the torpedo fish. We shall mention other dramatic features shortly, but first let us ask whether the text suggests any generalization that might be applied to all of Meno's unsuccessful efforts. Such a suggestion is indeed provided in Socrates' objection to Meno's final effort to define virtue. He objects to the definition as *circular*, for he complains, at 79a, that he has asked for a definition of "virtue as a whole" and that Meno has answered that "whatever is accompanied by justice or honesty is virtue"; and, says Socrates, these are only *parts* of virtue. He finally asks, "Can anyone who does not know virtue know a part of virtue?"[38]

---

[38] What is wrong with a circular definition becomes obvious as soon as one considers the purpose of a definition. The purpose of a definition is to make a word, term, or idea clear—or "definite"; it uses other words, terms, or ideas to accomplish this. What is to be defined is called the *definiendum*; what accomplishes the definition is the *definiens*. In a successful definition the *definiendum* is made definite by the *definiens*; or the clarity of the former

There can be little doubt that the dialogue has here reached a crucial point. In addition to the dramatic features already mentioned that give emphasis to it the reader should note some others. This point represents the end of Meno's efforts to define virtue. In fact, after what is sometimes called a "dramatic interlude" he drops out of the dialogue, giving place to his slave boy; when he re-enters (rather briefly) he refuses to resume the efforts to define virtue. Second, Meno's frustration is the occasion for one of Socrates' famous presentations of Plato's "doctrine of recollection." Third, what Meno has just offered as a definition is criticized not only as invalid but as an interruption of the progress of the dialogue. For Socrates says, "I gave you a pattern" (the definition of *figure*); Meno has failed to follow it.

These features call attention to the end of Meno's struggles with the problem of definition rather than to the other problem which Meno poses at this time: How will you inquire into that which you do not know? The new problem is itself a formidable philosophical difficulty, and it would be easy for the reader to become engrossed in it. It does not seem that Plato wants us to do so. He does not want the new problem itself to receive much attention; he wants it to introduce a new phase of the discussion of the problem of definition. If we recognize this dividing point between two distinct phases we should also be asking how the two phases are interrelated, that is, we should be concerned with the structure of the dialogue.

At the same time, readers should not go too far (as they often do) in minimizing the philosophical importance of Meno's new problem. If we are to make the best case for Meno,[39] we should consider that when he says, "And how will you inquire, Socrates,

---

depends upon the clarity of the latter. In a circular definition this dependency is reversed: the *definiens* is not clear without reference to something already included in the *definiendum*. If this is so, nothing has been accomplished by the definition: we are right back where we were before we tried to define; we have traveled in a circle.

[39] To do less than this for any of Socrates' interlocutors only makes Socrates' refutations that much less significant.

into that which you do not know?" he is not creating an irrelevant diversion but is trying to meet the objection Socrates has made just before: that Meno's last definition is circular. We should not, perhaps, credit Meno with a full understanding of the implications of his question, which could be said to entail questions such as: If it is argued that the knowledge of the whole is prior to knowledge of the part, is this so without qualification? Is the knowledge of the whole absolutely independent of knowledge of the part? Is there such a thing as a simply virtuous act, or are not all virtuous acts either just or temperate or courageous, and so on? The importance of these philosophical questions should not be minimized, but if the reader becomes preoccupied with them he may find that he is no longer reading the *Meno*, and that is what we are now engaged in doing. How does the *Meno* suggest that we proceed with our reflections? That is to say, what does the dialogue make of this philosophical difficulty?

First, is it not correct that the dialogue is not directly interested in the new problem as Meno expresses it? When he asks, "And is not the argument sound?" Socrates merely replies, "I think not." He never directly attacks the soundness of Meno's skeptical argument. He turns instead to the "doctrine of recollection," which seems to some readers to concede Meno's point, that we never really do acquire knowledge, but only recall it.[40] Second, does not the statement that "all learning is but recollection" evoke in us, as it did in Meno, the desire to have this process convincingly demonstrated? This is the direction in which the dialogue moves.

If we attribute primary importance to the movement of the dialogue, rather than to the particular problems or conclusions that are brought forward in it at one point or another, we will willingly

---

[40] We have to do here with one of the disputed points in the interpretation of Plato. One school thinks that Plato's meaning is literal: that when we "learn" we really do recollect knowledge that we had in some previous existence. The other school thinks Plato is here using a figure of speech which is intended to indicate that our acquisition of knowledge requires something that is in some sense prior to experience, not derived from it. I take the latter position.

follow Plato's lead and move on to the slave boy episode, without pausing to struggle directly with Meno's difficulty. But before leaving the latter altogether, we might add two reflections. First, even if we do not rescue Meno from his predicament, does the order of things in the dialogue not tell us that he fell into it because he was unable to follow the pattern Socrates provided for him? The fact that one lands in hopeless difficulties may be taken as an indication that one's mode of thinking is basically wrong, and that he should make a fresh start. Many later philosophers have expressed this idea by refusing to grapple with some of the traditional puzzles of philosophy; they have argued that the puzzles exist only because problems have not been properly formulated and that the best thing to do is to find a new start in formulating them. Second, the reader may find, before he is through with this and other Platonic dialogues, that the part-whole impasse that has baffled Meno is not really forgotten by Plato, and, in fact, that the problems of learning and of becoming virtuous have everything to do with working out part-whole relationships.

Up to the point where Meno describes Socrates as a torpedo fish the dialogue can be subdivided into three small parts. First (71e–75b) (after an introduction which substitutes Socrates' question, What is virtue? for Meno's, How is virtue acquired?), Meno takes the lead (he offers answers to Socrates' question) and suggests two definitions of virtue; although he is in one sense the leader in this part of the dialogue, his suggestions are severely criticized or refuted by Socrates, who really dominates the discussion. Second (75b–77b), Socrates openly takes the lead by offering answers to the question, What is figure? (as well as to the related question, What is color?); here it is Meno who is the critic, but Socrates still dominates. Third (77b–80b), Meno resumes the answering role, and returns to the question, What is virtue? We have already given some attention to the result.

In the interest of brevity we are not going to pay detailed attention to the first and third of these subdivisions. The omission is, however, serious; for it is important to understand why Meno falls into the difficulty we have discussed. Unless this is understood one cannot see the necessity of the significantly different approach represented in the discussion with the slave boy.

Let us turn to the second subdivision. In it Socrates is not merely critical of someone else, but offers positive suggestions of his own. We may therefore hope to find in it some of Plato's own ideas about inquiry. It gives us three definitions, and it indicates clearly that Meno prefers one of them, the third; he is dissatisfied with the first, and apparently accepts the second, but without enthusiasm. Socrates, however, thinks "the other" was better than the third one, which Meno preferred. Although it is not expressly indicated that "the other" is the second ("figure is the limit of solid"), this must be what is meant, since it seems to be regarded as preferable to the first ("figure is the only thing which always follows color").

None of these definitions is circular; so they are all better than any of Meno's. But how are they ranked by Socrates, and why are they ranked as they are? What is clearest about their ranking is that the second is better than the first and the third. The first is criticized for being "such a simple answer." Is a complex definition better than a simple one? Not necessarily, for the second definition is just as simple as the first; yet Socrates puts it forward as an improvement, and Meno accepts it. But Meno's fondness for complexity is reflected in his preference for the third definition ("color is an effluence of form, commensurate with sight, and palpable to sense"). But Socrates prefers the second to the third; and this may mean that he thinks the simple definition is the better definition. But if this is so, why does Socrates prefer the second to the first? They seem to be equally simple.

Why, then, is the second definition better than the first? Meno's second criticism of the first definition was that it would not help anyone who said he did not know what color was. Is the second definition any better on this score? Not in itself, perhaps, because the same person might say, with reference to the second definition, that he did not know what solid was. In spite of this similarity between the first and second definitions, the way in which Socrates moves toward the second is different. The first is directly stated, and the person who hears it is free to say that he does not understand one of its terms. The second is not directly stated, but is developed step by step; no new step is made until "the person interrogated [is] willing to admit" each premise as it is introduced. The person who says he understands *limit* and *solid* must understand a definition in which these are the key terms. The idea implicit in all this is: no definition or argument can be simply and directly considered by itself; the manner in which it is developed, and the states of mind of those who are following the discussion are what is important. (This confirms the procedure we have been following, according to which Meno's great perplexity is less important in itself than how he fell into it; and it is the latter question that we are now exploring.)

If there were no other difference between the first and second definitions than the manner in which they are developed, and the willingness or unwillingness of "the person interrogated" to admit one step or another, we should be tempted to conclude that the value of a definition is entirely relative to the caprices of the persons interrogated. There are, however, many indications in the dialogues of Plato that what a person is willing to admit is not a matter of caprice, but a matter of the kind of person he really is. It is because Meno and the slave boy are the kinds of persons they are that they respond differently to the questioning of Socrates.

What kinds of persons could say, "I do not know what color is"? An "eristic and antagonistic" sort could say it, not because he really did not know, but in order to create a sophistic difficulty. If a blind man were to say it, however, it would be a sincere response, and we should have to abandon *color* as a term, if we wanted to define figure for him. The eristic and antagonistic person could also say he did not know what solid was. But can there be anyone for whom solidity is as meaningless as color is to a blind man? If not, then the meaning of solid is really clearer than the meaning of color, and the second definition is really superior to the first; because, in the second definition the term to be defined is related to defining ideas whose clarity is not a matter of mere opinion.

Our first reaction to the third definition might be to notice that it contains many fancy terms, and that each of these (unlike *solid*, or even *color*) seems to be in need of definition. Meno is "the person interrogated," and it fits his character, because it sounds so grand—the first page of the dialogue indicates that he has little interest in knowledge for its own sake. But it would be unfair to Meno to say no more than this. He has probably studied the theories of Empedocles, and the terms of the third definition may therefore be clear to him; so, he could have good reason to "be willing to admit them." But the definition would be meaningless to someone not versed in the Empedoclean theory. The best that can be said for it is that it might have some value if the terms which it relates to the term *color* are themselves related to many other terms, until a system of relationships is built up in which all the terms are understood. But it is hardly a good definition with which to begin constructing such a system. Would it not be possible for a blind man to be taught the Empedoclean theory (about effluent particles that correspond to sense receptor organs), and to be convinced that "there is such a thing as sight"? Yet, would he really learn what color is through that definition?

At this point the reader should somehow take his bearings and ask what he can conclude from the Socratic treatment of the problem of definition. Ordinarily he should, at such a point, try to formulate the conclusion in words, and he should try to do so here. No philosopher, however, is more difficult to summarize or paraphrase than Plato. We have already seen that our initial summary of the fragment from the *Meno* gives us less of the substance of what Plato teaches than we learn about Hume in a corresponding summary. Suppose we now say that definition, if it is to be effective, must relate the idea to be defined to other ideas that are more clear. The statement is not incorrect, but it is meaningful only to someone who can see how *solid* is more clear than *color*, and *color* more clear than *effluence*. And he could see these things better through the dialogue itself than through any explanatory words.

We might elaborate our explanation by adding that the clearest ideas (which do the defining) are not less clear to some persons and more clear to others and that they do not depend upon special theories which are more complicated than the problem for which the definition is needed. Again, these additional statements may be on the right track, but they cry out for qualifications (e.g., in what sense are really clear ideas clear to all persons alike?) and for additional explanation; and we feel that we should be better off without these qualifications and that we should simply return to the dialogue (if we still do not see the point clearly), or turn to some other problem and apply the point to it—hoping that we have grasped the point well enough to be able to use it and expecting to test our grasp by our success or failure in using it.

The Doctrine of Recollection

Let us turn now to the doctrine of recollection, which is introduced in the long paragraph at 81b. When (p. 129 above) we listed three shortcomings of our summary statement, it was the second of these that concerned recollection. During our reflections on the first shortcoming our interest in the structure of the dialogue became sharpened. Now we have more reason than ever to reflect on the paragraph at 81b. If we can understand it better, and find how it is related to the problem of definition (which comes before it) and to the slave boy episode (which follows it and which is the subject of the third "shortcoming" of our statement), the structure of our entire fragment may be illuminated. Let us approach the "recollection" paragraph from the point we reached in discussing Meno's difficulties with definition. We formulated the conclusion (unsatisfactorily, to be sure) by saying that we can be brought to understand ideas by relating them to other ideas that are more clear. In the recollection paragraph this point is extended: since "all nature is akin" (i.e., since everything is related to everything else), we can trace all of nature's relationships if, with some clear relationships in mind, we can approach nature and grasp some part of it by means of that clear relationship; we must, on the one hand, have such a starting point, and, on the other hand, we must be active and inquisitive in expanding our understanding of the interrelationships in nature. The ideal is to come to an understanding of nature as a whole. Our brief explanation of Plato can scarcely suggest how that can be completed, but it can give us the first thing we would want, a demonstration of how it is possible to acquire new knowledge by applying, to new experience, a relationship we have already firmly grasped.

The Slave Boy Episode

What does the slave boy already know clearly, as Socrates begins to question him? Aside from the meaning of certain words like *line* and *square*, and the number system, he knows what *equality* is, and what *double* and *half* are. *Equal* and *double* both refer to relationships. Where did he acquire his understanding of these relationships? The point of the Platonic doctrine of recollection is that we cannot point to any occasion in his life on which he learned them; they were somehow in his mind whenever he had occasion to consider whether two things were equal, or whether one thing was double another. We will mark only two crucial points in the discussion. The first is at 84b, where the slave boy says, "Indeed, Socrates, I do not know." This is a confession Meno is never able to make. The slave boy is willing to make it because, for one thing, he does not have Meno's pride, and, for another, he knows that the possibilities he has thus far explored do not harmonize with ideas he already thinks he understands. Second, the boy resolves his problem when he recognizes a new way to divide a square into two equal parts—by drawing a diagonal from one corner to another. There is no trick here, as some readers are inclined to suspect (they doubt Socrates' claim that he has "taught" the boy nothing). The operation of drawing the diagonal has not occurred to him; Socrates draws it for him. But the boy *sees* that the operation results in two *equal* parts. Socrates does indeed ask him, "And does not this line, reaching from corner to corner, bisect each of these spaces?" But the boy's "Yes" must be taken to mean that he himself really sees that this is so—he is not simply accepting what Socrates tells him. Since the boy knows that eight is twice four and half of sixteen, and since he knows that the original square now has four spaces, so that its double must have eight and its half two; and since he knows that four such halves will give him the eight he wants; and, finally, since he now sees that the diagonal will give him such a two-unit half, he can construct the double square he was looking for. The demonstration is over.

III

If he is adequately to develop his capacity to read philosophy the reader should of course broaden his philosophical experience. His further reading should include works significantly different from those of Hume and Plato. In the final section of this chapter the primary reference will be John Dewey's *Human Nature and Conduct*. In approaching this book the reader will find it useful to raise questions like those that have already been suggested. In this brief discussion of Dewey, I shall try to bring out some features that distinguish him (and other writers who resemble him, notably Aristotle) from Hume and Plato.

Dewey's *Human Nature and Conduct* has been selected because of significant ways in which it differs from the books of Hume and Plato. More generally, there is value in considering a work written in our own century, two centuries after Hume; as a result, the reader will have had presented to him, in this chapter, one ancient work and one contemporary work, and one work which is neither. Also, the subjects of the three books have something in common, for all the differences that must be noted. All three are concerned with virtue or morality, and how these qualities are developed. Comparison based on this common subject will, it is hoped, make differences in thinking and writing stand in relief.[41]

In the mode of philosophizing exemplified here by Dewey the

---

[41] The reader may wish to proceed with some study of Dewey, but wonder whether he might not do so with a shorter book. This particular book has been chosen because its subject relates it so well to the books by Hume and Plato. It is hoped, however, that our brief introduction to Deweyan thought will enable a reader to turn to a shorter book by Dewey, and to make good progress in understanding it. He might well choose *The Public and Its Problems*, or *A Common Faith*, both much shorter than *Human Nature and Conduct*, and solidify his grasp of Dewey through one of them. Before doing so, however, he is urged to read more of the longer volume, including its table of contents, along with the remaining text of the present essay.

principle—that to which everything else is ultimately referred—is some fundamental relationship. In a relationship there are at least two terms (*term* is not used here in the linguistic sense), each of which is, as a member of the relationship, nothing by itself. The relationship of parent and child is an illustration: neither parent nor child is, as a member of this relationship, anything without reference to the other term in the relationship. In philosophy such a relationship can serve as a starting point either for analysis or for synthesis. That is, the relationship can be anlayzed or broken down into its related terms; or, we may synthesize by combining one relationship with another, so as to produce another relationship of a higher order. Understanding is increased by both these processes. We do not really understand any given parent and child relationship unless we are able to distinguish the parent from the child; and our understanding grows if we are able to put together two parent and child relationships and produce another relationship, such as that of grandparent and grandchild.[42]

In themselves the illustrations fail to show how Dewey's mode of thinking differs from Hume's and Plato's, because the terms that loom large in their thinking are also related to other terms. But something distinctive can be seen in Dewey if he is compared with Hume. The virtue of benevolence is a component part of personal merit, in which a good many other qualities are related to one another. Hume does not, however, explore the relationship in which all the qualities stand, except to say that they all are approved of. But this fact does not require that they be thought of in relation with one another. It is possible to take any one of the qualities by

---

[42] The example is not altogether satisfactory, because the terms *grandparent*, *grandchild*, *parent*, and *child* all refer to entities of the same kind: we should say that all four are human beings, or perhaps, animals or plants. Therefore no term seems to be uniquely what it is only in the relationship in which it immediately stands. Yet, it can be so taken, and if it is, it remains correct to say that although a parent is a human being, just what it is as a parent is not indicated by the term *human being*. The term *generation* comes closer to indicating the new relationship brought to attention when we relate two sets of parents and children (but parents and children can be related to other entities in an infinite number of ways.)

itself and say that it is approved of; no reference to any other approved quality is necessary when this is said. Furthermore, after all the meritorious qualities have been isolated, Hume tries to reduce them all to one and comes to the conclusion that morality is founded upon benevolence. He tends, then, to think of the quality of benevolence by itself as in irreducible element without which there could be no morality. It is true, as Dewey might wish to say, that benevolence has no meaning by itself; it is intelligible only in terms of a relationship involving a benevolent person, on the one hand, and a benefited person, on the other. Hume would not need to deny this, although it is interesting to notice that he pays little attention to this fact. But for us it is especially interesting to recall that he takes benevolent feeling out of its immediate relationship with the object of that feeling, and places it in another relationship, the spectator relationship, which he insists is a different relationship. But in spite of the difference the quality of benevolence is considered to be substantially the same in both relationships; and this would be what Dewey would tend to question.[43]

For Plato any given idea can be understood only in relation to

---

[43] This interpretation may be debated, because it can be argued that Hume does not, as I have implied, reach an ultimate principle which is what it is, regardless of the relationships it stands in with other things. Attention could be called, for example, to the first note to Section V, of *An Inquiry concerning the Principles of Morals*, where Hume says, "A very small variation of the object, even where the same qualities are preserved, will destroy a sentiment. Thus the same beauty, transferred to a different sex, excites no amorous passion where nature is not extremely perverted." I will not dispute the argument, except to say that even here Hume thinks the qualities may be the same in different objects, even though they may enter into different relations (beauty being related to some things in sexual love, and to other things in other contexts). I should prefer to concede the argument, and to point out that what I am now engaged in doing is to call attention to differences of emphasis, rather than sharp differences in kind. "Pure" examples of one kind of philosophizing or another probably do not exist. Or, if they do, they are probably not very strong modes of thinking. In what follows it is implicitly recognized, throughout, that Hume, Plato, and Dewey share the very features being used to contrast them, but that these features receive very different emphases in the three thinkers.

other ideas. So far we could not say that he differs from Dewey. But Plato, through Socrates, bids us be active and inquisitive, to be strenuous and not to "faint," in our effort to increase our understanding of any of the ideas we can partially grasp, by tracing out the relationships in which they stand to everything else. The reader might think that the slave boy has reached an adequate knowledge of one function of the diagonal of the square; but Socrates says, after the boy has "solved" his problem, "at present these notions have just been stirred up in him, as in a dream." Plato would say (if we take liberties with chronology) that even one who has mastered Euclid does not really understand Euclidean geometry; he would also think that our understanding of Euclidean geometry would be more adequate if we understood other geometric systems and were able to place them in intelligible relationships with the system of Euclid.

It is usually comparatively easy, with thinkers like Dewey, to see the fundamental relationships that underlie their thinking, because so much reference is made to these relationships in the relevant writings: *experience, interaction, situation,* in Dewey; *substance and accident, potentiality and actuality,* in Aristotle. It is less easy to see how these relationships are put to work; and unless this is seen not much is learned. Abstractly formulated suggestions are not of much help, and we shall rely chiefly, in the final part of this section, on an examination of a concrete piece of philosophical thinking, in Dewey's work. Dewey analyzes an enormous variety of problems in ways that relate readily to his analysis of experience. He holds that interactions take place at many levels of complexity, and that these many levels constitute a continuous hierarchy in which the more complex evolve from the less complex. A common pattern can be found at all levels, and that is why it is possible, if one has made an effective analysis at a comparatively simple level, to learn to apply the distinctions and relationships derived from the simple level to the problems found at higher levels.

Dewey differs from Plato because his investigations of any given problem center definitely upon that problem and resolve it by carrying out a sufficient analysis with reference to his fundamental analysis of experience and life. It is not necessary to relate that particular investigation to the highest levels of human activity. For Plato any given investigation falls significantly short of its goal to the extent that it fails to be related to the highest human concerns. For Dewey it is sufficient to take one problem at a time, and if there are other problems which must be considered in its investigation, they are problems less complex than the one that is his immediate concern, problems from which the problem at hand—the one being investigated—has emerged.[44]

This mode of philosophizing is characteristically very much concerned with the definition of the subject of each inquiry. It is this concern that most obviously sets this philosophy apart from Platonism. We have noted how, at the beginning of Plato's *Meno*, the subject appears to be the acquisition of virtue; how this quickly changes to the problem of defining virtue; how definition itself becomes the object of study; and how, at the conclusion of the fragment we studied, the dialogue returns to the original question, when Meno says, "I would much rather return to my original question." This very return accentuates the fact that the first effort to inquire into it has led us to inquire into other subjects of a wide range and vast complexity.

Dewey and Aristotle, early in their inquiries, devote careful attention to determining their subjects. One effect of this limitation is to keep the inquiry sharply focused, to prevent it from losing itself in tangential matters. It is perhaps more important that the effort to delimit the subject goes hand in hand with an effort to find the method of inquiry most appropriate to it; and that is to find the specification of general method which best applies, to this

---

[44] For example, it is more necessary, in the investigation of problems of psychology, to investigate basic problems of biology than to investigate problems of morals. Still, one could maintain that in book after book Dewey is concerned to bring his inquiry to the point where it can illuminate one particular kind of problem—the problem of morals and civilization. This is because he was primarily a moral philosopher. He consistently maintains that the method he advocates for the social and moral sciences is basically the same method as that actually employed by natural scientists, and that the only differences are modifications demanded by differences of subject matter.

particular problem, the modes of analysis each thinker takes to be most fundamental. This can be differently expressed (in language borrowed from Dewey's *Logic, the Theory of Inquiry*) by saying that both the *ultimate* and the *proximate* subject matter of the inquiry must be defined, and the one related to the other. The proximate subject matter of an inquiry is what many inquirers are likely to agree about, even if they are of different philosophical schools: for example, the proximate subject matter of logic includes inferences, and the interrelations of propositions and terms; the proximate subject matter of esthetics is paintings, poems, symphonies, and the like. For Dewey the ultimate subject matter of both logic and esthetics is the structure of experience. It is characteristic of Dewey to turn his attention first to the ultimate subject matter of his inquiry, and then to find that that subject matter has to be analyzed so that the analysis can illuminate the particular problem we have at hand, which is our proximate subject matter.

We shall now analyze Section I, "Habits as Social Functions," of Part One, "The Place of Habit in Conduct," of Dewey's *Human Nature and Conduct*. This section, which is reprinted at the back of this book, has only eleven paragraphs. Its brevity lends itself well to a procedure that may appear pedestrain: going through the section paragraph by paragraph, trying to see what the function of each paragraph is, and how all eleven paragraphs go together as a beginning of the inquiry to which the whole book is devoted. Such a procedure is not to be reserved only for books of this particular kind. The reader of philosophy should find it useful with many instances of philosophical writing. I illustrate its use on this particular text because the text responds so well to it. One important reason why it works well on Dewey is that it enables the reader to obtain a firm grasp on the fundamental relationship, or set of relationships, on which the entire book is constructed. If this grasp is truly firm, the rest of the book is comparatively easy to read; if is is not, even a great deal of effort will not prevent the reader from going astray.

In the first paragraph *habit*, the subject of Part One, is said to be like a physiological function. This is an indication that physiological processes present a model, or point of reference, with reference to which any given subject, or at least this one, is to be understood. Physiological functions exemplify the relationship which is fundamental in all Dewey's writings, the relationships between an organism and its environment. He emphasizes that each of these terms is of equal importance in the relationship—that each is, in the relationship, what it is by virtue of the relation it has to the other term. One cannot know what an organism is apart from the environment the organism needs in order to be that organism. The particular environment that that organism needs is that environment only in relation to that organism. A corresponding statement can be made about each function of an organism: for each function there is some corresponding environmental factor, and vice versa.

The first paragraph emphasizes the role of the environmental factors. There are rhetorical reasons for the emphasis: Dewey assumes that the reader is likely to attribute physiological functions and habits to the organism and to overlook the importance of the environment; he therefore emphasizes the environmental side, although it is clear that he attributes equal importance to each side.

The emphasis on the environment is strongest with reference to moral discussion. This special stress indicates, on the one hand, that Dewey finds a problem in the present state of moral discussion, because the role of environment in morals has not been duly recognized. It also indicates this problem is the problem of this particular book. A full idea of the problem, so far as it can be gathered from this paragraph, involves attention to habit in conduct, and to the bearing of environmental factors upon habit.

Dewey has now given us some indication of the reason for inquiring into the subject of Part One, "The Place of Habit in Conduct." It would help the reader, before he moves on, to know that Part Two is "The Place of Impulse in Conduct," and Part Three "The Place of Intelligence in Conduct." He should be alert, then, for Dewey's ways of interrelating habit, impulse, and intelligence, which seem to be the terms he uses most in working out the relations between human nature and conduct.

The second paragraph reinforces the point about the importance of environmental factors to habit, by comparing habits with arts. Dewey thinks the reader can see in the arts the same bipolar structure that physiological functions have, and he thinks it is clear that art, like physiological functions, depends upon environmental factors.

The rhetorical reasons for stressing environmental factors are indicated in paragraph three, with special reference to accepted ways of thinking about morals, ways Dewey intends to challenge. An additional point may be derived from this paragraph, one that has been operating before but that stands out more here: we are concerned with a process, and concern with and attention to a process requires that we should not isolate one factor from another, because the process is one that connects these factors—the process is an interaction, and when we view it thus we are prevented from taking one of the interacting elements out of the interactive process and considering it by itself, as is done when character is separated from conduct, which is a process.

In the latter part of paragraph three the connection of morality (viewed as activity of a very high level) with the earth displays the continuity Dewey always insists on, in interrelating various levels of interaction. The reference to "honesty, chastity, malice" reminds us that we are seeing Dewey's way of dealing with the same subject matter Hume dealt with (and Plato too, though less clearly so). The last four sentences illustrate (with reference to habit, his proximate subject matter in this section) Dewey's characteristic way of viewing every subject in terms of the organism-environment relationship; for example, "They [virtues and vices] are interactions of elements contributed by the make-up of an individual with elements supplied by the out-door world."

In the fourth paragraph the reader can see how the analysis of habit, which has been simplified so as to stress the similarity between habit (a comparatively complex function) and physiological functions (which are simpler), can be complicated so as to become more adequate for the understanding of human conduct. Dewey implicitly recognizes that habits are more complex than physiological functions. He tells us in this paragraph that habits involve environing conditions that are social, not just physical. The social environment is more complicated than an environment of merely physical forces, because the constituent elements of a social situation share what is involved.[45]

It follows very naturally from the concept of sharing, in paragraph five, that responsibility belongs not only to the individual but also to those who make up the environing society. The point Dewey makes here is that any reaction we have to what other people do can have some effect on the habits they form. The context of an individual's actions is expanded when the members of his society share responsibility for what he does. But Dewey does not wish his readers to oversimplify this expansion, as the conclusion of the paragraph shows. Because they share responsibility the members of society are added to what would otherwise be an environment of merely impersonal forces; but when it comes to conduct, the members of the society are not the only important environmental factors. Other factors are still there and should not be forgotten. It will not do simply to react against, say, a criminal, as a member of our society; our reaction must take into account (and the role of intelligence[46] is here anticipated) all environmental factors which can be "causes of criminality." It is also indicated that our reactions must be guided by considering the consequences of our reaction on the character (habits) of the criminal.

Two features of paragraph six deserve comment. First, by recognizing the importance of both poles of the situation (here the individual and society) we can recognize failures to take both into consideration. The individual blames society for what he himself does; society reciprocates by blaming the individual. Both are one-sided views, which are continually objects of Dewey's attacks.

---

[45] *Situation* is Dewey's favorite word for the whole which is constituted of organic and environmental factors. The concept of sharing receives much attention in his writings, but we will not go into it here, assuming that it conveys enough meaning for Dewey's present purposes.

[46] Recall the references to Parts Two and Three, on p. 145, above.

Second, and more important for this paragraph, the failure to take account of both poles is a failure of intelligence (again, an anticipation of Part Three), which should be concerned with control of the future. When an individual blames society for his troubles, he entertains no possibility of any change in himself which can improve the future; correspondingly, when society blames the individual, without taking account of the social forces that have contributed to make him what he is, and of the effect upon him of anything like punitive reaction, improvement is not likely to take place in the future.

The sixth paragraph's emphasis upon the future warrants giving special attention to the third sentence, "Questions of causation are physical, not moral except when they concern future consequences." Causation is an important concept for Dewey, as it is for many philosophers. The distinction between physical and moral causation should be noted here and interpreted in the light of what has been said about Dewey. *Causation*, the term common to physical causation and moral causation, refers to a process with a pattern common to both. The difference between the two is a consequence of introducing, into the common pattern, an additional element that makes one more complex than the other: moral causation is more complex than physical. The additional element is concern for the future consequences, as our sentence says. A little reflection will show that concern for future consequences can be an additional element in causation only when future consequences (which do not physically exist in the present) can become causal factors. They can become controlling factors only through the introduction of intelligence, the subject of Part Three.

At the end of paragraph six the past and the future have emerged as poles of a temporal process. Do they mark out terms that are related to each other reciprocally, as are organism and environment? At first glance we would think not, for the past influences the future, but not the future the past. But in paragraph seven there is another anticipation of intelligence. In the mind, ideas acquired from past experience do interact with ideas that are "prospective." And here the interaction is reciprocal. Our past experience has its significance modified by our prospective glances, which are, in turn, continually developed with reference to what the past has taught us. It is upon this sort of interaction among ideas that intelligent control of conduct depends. Application of the pattern of physiological functions to the past-future distinction might be pressed further. Could we not say that the mind, as a fund of meanings that have been acquired from past experience, is organic? and the prospective view of the future a "venturing forth" (in Deweyan language) into the environment?

Paragraph eight continues to develop the place of intelligence in conduct and to relate intelligence to the place of habit in conduct. It notes that ideas which are common in ordinary life support the stress that has been placed on the part social factors play in the formation of habits. But it contrasts the usual use of these ideas with an intelligent use of them. When Dewey says, "We cannot change habit directly," he confirms what has been said about the need for intelligent consideration of the environmental factors that condition the formation of habits; and he elaborates on this remark in what follows in Section II, "Habits and Will."

The idea of the interrelation (and even interaction) of past and present in intelligent human experience is capable of expansion beyond the limits of a single human life, and this expansion is introduced in paragraph nine. The idea of civilization is treated here as a vast expansion of the ideas of mind and intelligence: "Our individual habits are links in forming the endless chain of humanity." Notice here that one of Dewey's basic means (perhaps his most basic) of developing the simple or primitive notion of interaction, developing it so that it can illuminate the most complex levels, entails the use of the dimension of time (as in paragraphs six and seven, with the introduction of the future, and then of concern for the future). It is of course necessarily entailed by the idea of process, for processes take time. It is not, simply that time is required for a process to take place; it is the possibility of utilizing a vast amount of past experience and of controlling our activities by intelligent foresight that makes it possible for men to bring civilization to complex and lofty heights.

In the last two paragraphs, in considering how we as individuals can actually serve as links in "the endless chain of humanity,"

Dewey stresses the consequences of what we do, respectively, on our environment, and on "personal or subjective factors." In the stress on the former, in paragraph ten, we see an interesting contrast with Hume in such remarks as, "no amount of preaching good will or the golden rule or cultivation of sentiments of love and equity will accomplish the results. There must be change in objective arrangements and institutions. We must work on the environment not merely on the hearts of men." The paragraph also reminds us that—since habit is not simply a possession belonging to a person, but involves interaction with environmental factors—when changes in objective conditions endure, habits too endure.

Paragraph eleven with its initial stress on "personal or subjective factors," helps to balance paragraph ten. But it moves on to, and concludes appropriately with, an effort to give equal importance to both these and to environmental factors, and to take one further analytic step. It begins to indicate different functions that are performed by the environmental or personal factors, respectively—functions that are different but of comparable importance: "Desire for flowers comes after actual enjoyment of flowers. But it comes before the work that makes the desert blossom. . . ." Desire for flowers is, of course, what Dewey is calling a personal factor; and flowers, which must be there before actual enjoyment, are environmental. Desire for flowers may occur on a merely physical level, when flowers grow naturally, and desire grows naturally out of their enjoyment. But when that desire becomes effective (i.e., causal) in making the desert blossom, the realm of morality has been entered.

In this concluding passage the personal organism and the environment are neatly brought into relation with the past and future poles of the processes of refined life. A pattern according to which the inquiry can proceed has been presented by Dewey with considerable richness (for so brief a chapter), and one who reads the remainder of the book can see how the pattern is, on the one hand, continually modified and complicated, and, on the other hand, continually reverted to in order to keep the inquiry under control.

Chapter 5

Rhetoric

The study of the rhetorical aspects of literature should be guided from the outset by a realization that there are two kinds of writing, not absolute kinds, but distinguished from each other by their rhetorical characteristics. First, there are the works most obviously rhetorical, such as speeches. Second, and more important for the reader's total experience, there are all the other works of literature, non-rhetorical in purpose but none without its rhetorical aspect. Works of history, drama, fiction, or philosophy may be fully understood only if the reader learns to understand the place of rhetoric in them. This chapter is based on the idea that practice in analyzing works of the first class can develop the reading disciplines appropriate not only for such works but also for understanding the rhetorical characteristics of other works. We shall accordingly be directly concerned with analyzing a work written as a speech, Pericles' *Funeral Oration*, as it is given to us by Thucydides.[1] Following this analysis, we shall see how it may help us interpret works of history, drama, fiction, and philosophy.

Study of the use of rhetoric in works most thoroughly rhetorical in form can do much to bring the reader to a complete understanding also of their structure and substance. In works where the use of rhetoric is ancillary, though by no means unimportant, some other aspect must be relied on to accomplish the same end. The

---

[1] This chapter is intended to be read along with Pericles' *Funeral Oration*, as it is found in chapters 35-46 of Book II of Thucydides' *History of the Peloponnesian War*. Alfred Zimmern's translation of this speech, from his book *The Greek Commonwealth* (5th ed.; London: Oxford University Press, 1931) is reprinted as an appendix to this book (pp. 182-89).

line between the two kinds of works is not a sharp one. It would be more accurate to consider literature along a continual axis representing the use of rhetoric. At one pole would be what I call the first kind—pieces essentially rhetorical. Other works would be more or less distant from this pole, depending upon the extent to which they could be fully interpreted without reference to rhetorical considerations. Generally speaking, rhetoric is more important in fiction than in philosophy, but this generalization is very rough, since some particular works of philosophy are more "rhetorical" than some particular novels.

Probably the most famous treatise on the subject is Aristotle's *Rhetoric*. Rhetoric, says Aristotle at the outset, has no subject matter; any subject may be treated rhetorically. In form he seems to consider it as a kind of literary composition—very close to what we call a speech. In considering a speech we think of the speaker as an individual, the speech itself, and the particular audience. In these aspects a speech differs markedly from a work of philosophy. The writer of a philosophical work is indeed an individual, but his individual personality tends to be submerged, in contrast to that of the speech-maker. The particular character of the philosophical "audience" is even more submerged. Philosophical writing is usually addressed not to any particular audience, but to human reason wherever it may be found.[2] As a result of these differences both speaker and audience (or reader) loom large in rhetorical considerations; their importance takes away some of the relative importance of the speech itself (or writing). The reverse is true of non-rhetorical literature. In philosophy we should naturally expect the substance of the writing itself to be far and away the main thing. Our normal expectation is the same in fiction: the story is the main thing, and it is only when we reflect upon it, on a comparatively sophisticated level, that we consider how the author is telling the story, and how his telling is oriented toward the kind of readers he expects or wants.

---

[2] This is true in Plato's dialogues too. Even though the idiosyncrasies of Meno and those of his slave boy should be taken into account, the boy, immature and untaught as he is, represents human reason in its universality better than his master Meno does.

Aristotelian students of rhetoric give special emphasis to the effect that the speaker intends to have upon his audience. Accordingly, they divide speeches into three classes: *deliberative*, in which the speaker seeks to persuade his audience to undertake a particular course of action; *forensic*, in which he seeks to persuade the audience—characteristically a judge or jury—to pass judgment upon what some man has done; and *epideictic*, in which he seeks to arouse the approval or disapproval of something—to get his audience to praise or blame something or someone. Deliberative rhetoric has an important reference to future action, forensic to past action, and epideictic to something present.

In spite of the great influence of Aristotle, other thinkers have not been willing to confine rhetoric to the areas of deliberative, forensic, and epideictic oratory. They have given it a broader meaning which may be roughly suggested by the term *fine writing*. From antiquity to the present, children have been taught their "letters" in stages. The first stage has long been called "grammatical," and the second, "rhetorical." We still use the term *grammar school* when we speak of the place where children first learn the rudiments of reading and writing. Although the term *rhetoric* is no longer widely used in this context, it once meant the level of writing to which a young person would move after he had "learned his grammar."

In this sense of the word there is involved the idea that a person improves his understanding of letters when he reaches the level of rhetoric. He learns not just the terms and the structure of his language, but how to use it effectively. A person who succeeds at this level has learned to express himself, or to communicate with his readers: he has learned to say *what* he wants to say, *as* he wants to say it. He has, in this sense, now mastered the second of the liberal arts—grammar being the first.

The idea of rhetoric as a liberal art can be closely related to another broad use which has been given to the term during recent decades. In the consideration of the development of the art of fiction a very important mark of the level of artistry, in any given work, is the artist's success in obtaining just the effect he intended. Anyone can tell a story after a fashion, but some people tell one better than others. The best storytellers are skilful in knowing just how the story should be presented to the audience, and their skill lies in knowing just how a given effect upon an audience can best be produced. What the writer does toward this end may be more or less subtle, but any artistic storyteller keeps in mind the effect he wants to produce, and controls his writing accordingly.[3]

It was suggested above that rhetoric as such is of little importance in philosophy. The reader of philosophy might therefore think he should not consider it at all. But every writer of philosophy wishes to persuade his readers that what he says is true. He may attempt to idealize his reader to such an extent that the latter all but disappears from view—the reader becomes a personification of reason. The philosopher himself, however, is never this. What he writes, if it is worth writing at all, is something he thinks needs to be said, something that has not been said or thought before. To do this, he must in some way have in mind what *has* been thought before. He writes in the context of what has been thought before and to persuade someone to think as he has not thought before—someone who has thought in a way that the writer wishes to modify. It is more clear in some works of philosophy than in others that the writer has in mind readers whose particular thoughts and attitudes affect their response to his work. In Plato, for example, the proper names of the interlocutors, and of the various thinkers alluded to, make his concern for existing opinions evident. In other works it may not be so obvious, but philosophical writing in which reference to other writers is not explicitly or implicitly made are rare.[4]

---

[3] See Wayne C. Booth's *The Rhetoric of Fiction* (Chicago: University of Chicago Press, 1961), for a thorough presentation and criticism of examples of and theories about the role of rhetoric in fiction.

[4] Descartes is an interesting example. His *Meditations* purports to erase previous systems of philosophy from the board, and to begin anew from the foundations. Yet, apart from the fact that anyone who knows the history of philosophy can find in that book many covert allusions to doctrines held by earlier philosophers, it is significant that Descartes himself felt it very important to circulate his work among leading thinkers of his own time in order to get their comments and objections and that he published the latter, with his own replies, as part of the book.

Perhaps in all works of philosophy the authors make use of ideas which they assume that their readers accept, in order to move them to philosophical positions they have not previously held.

Just as the outward signs of rhetorical concern are more or less obvious, in different philosophies, so the rhetorical concerns of different philosophers differ a great deal in their intensity. It may be hard to find deliberative or epideictic purpose in a work like *Principia mathematica* by Bertrand Russell and Alfred North Whitehead. But a thinker like Dewey is intensely concerned that his thoughts have practical effects in the world. There is overwhelming evidence for this in his writings and in his career; and the reader will find it hard to overlook the rhetorical tone of what he says, even in such a "technical" work as *Logic, the Theory of Inquiry*. Or, one might turn to the more cloistered atmosphere in which we think the medieval philosophers wrote, and see—in St. Anselm, for example, or more notably perhaps in the vigorous and irascible character of St. Augustine—a profound hope that what is being written will affect the beliefs that control the way men live. Even in philosophy, then, the reader who wishes a thorough comprehension of what he reads cannot afford to neglect the rhetoric.

We shall begin our analysis of Thucydides' version of Pericles' *Funeral Oration* much as we began our analysis of Hume's *An Inquiry concerning the Principles of Morals:* we shall try to formulate a concise statement of the main point of the speech; with this main point in mind we shall try to work out a rough outline of the whole speech, in order to see how well its structure harmonizes with our summary statement; in making the summary and the rough outline we shall make use of any clues that may be explicit in the text; we should expect to find such clues in the introductory passages, and in fact we do, in chapters 35 and 36.[5] Pericles says

---

[5] In the standard form of reference to the parts of Thucydides' *History of the Peloponnesian War* the divisions marked by numbers in parentheses are called chapters. This analysis conforms to the standard and makes no reference to the paragraphing which—in the version included in this book— is that of the translator.

at the outset that he does not share the feeling "that solemn words should be spoken over our fallen soldiers." At the beginning of chapter 36 he says his "first words shall be for our ancestors." These words are few, however, and he indicates that he does not wish to say much "of the battles which we and our fathers fought." These remarks are not unlike the opening remarks of Hume's *Inquiry* and Plato's *Meno*, where it is indicated that certain questions either will not be pursued or will be deferred until others have been treated. The reader is thus prepared for Pericles' more positive indication of what he *is* going to do, what he thinks "it not unfitting" to call to mind, and "expedient too" for the gathering to listen to. "I wish rather," he says, "to set forth the spirit in which we faced them [the battles], and to pass from them to the dead."

We may well ask what significance Pericles' statement of his intentions has. This question is a fruitful one, for it will call attention to many things that are helpful in developing an interpretation of the speech. We may wonder first whether Pericles will in fact follow the stated order, speaking first of the spirit, then of the constitution and manners, and finally of the dead. And second we may wonder why he outlines his speech in this way, why he follows the order he does. Are the first topics intended to prepare for the last ones, or are the last ones merely elaborations of or supports for the first? The answer to this question is closely bound up with the problem of determining the main point of the speech. But Pericles hints at the answer when he says he does not feel that solemn words should be spoken over the fallen soldiers and indicates a special interest in speaking about the spirit, constitution, and manners of Athens.

The first question, Does the speech follow the stated sequence of topics? is more easily answered, and it should be answered early. In turning to it we find ourselves engaged in making a rough outline which may help us formulate our initial summary of the speech. Pericles does indeed defer speaking about the dead; but his first topic seems to be the *constitution*, not the *spirit*. A rough outline could run as follows:

Our second question, about Pericles' reasons for his order, is hard to answer at the beginning, and yet its answer would determine the nature of a summary speech. We shall therefore propose, not one summary statement, but two, assuming that there are two main alternatives between which we must decide. According to one interpretation our summary statement could run as follows:

1. Pericles sets forth the splendors of Athens in order to provide a basis for praising the soldiers who have fallen defending her.

A contrary interpretation might produce the following:

2. Pericles uses the state funeral as an occasion for praising the splendors of Athens. Each of his topics, including his remarks about the dead, is chosen to support that main purpose.

The use of two statements will not really complicate the task of analysis, because the analysis that supports one statement will be unfavorable to the other.

If we apply these statements to the text of the speech, questions of a familiar sort inevitably arise. Are there parts of the speech that do not seem accounted for by either statement? The two introductory chapters demand attention in the light of this question. As we have noted above, they imply that the second statement is more adequate than the first. The last three chapters also demand attention, because neither statement would have to be modified if chapters 44–46 were eliminated. But it still might be true that they fit one statement better than the other. Pericles' decision not to mourn, but only to offer comfort, fits the second better than the first. We shall return to the opening and concluding chapters later, but for the present we may simply note that they encourage us to adopt the second rather than the first summary statement.

There is another way, before making a detailed analysis, to find a suggestion about the main point of the speech. Let us imagine a reader who remembers little of the speech after he has read it, but who nevertheless does find it to some degree memorable. What is he likely to remember? I should think that what he would remember would be the splendid picture of Athens and her spirit. I am going to take this as another confirmation of the superiority of the second statement, because what is most memorable ought to be the main point, or closely related to it. This also we shall reflect upon later.

Let us turn now to what our outline has called Part II, the five chapters that follow chapter 36. They constitute about half of what remains after 35 and 36, and an even larger proportion of what might be regarded as the substance of the speech, if we take chapters 44–46 to be less substantive. An approach to a substantive part of a speech should be guided by an effort to discover some orderly pattern or patterns. Here it can also be governed by one of our provisional beliefs, that the spectacle of the splendor of Athens may be "the main point." Let us look first for orderly patterns, and see how the spectacle of Athens fits them.

It is not hard to find an orderly pattern in the beginning. Chapter 37 begins by calling attention to the democratic constitution of Athens, moves on to the social relations among the Athenians,[6] and, in connection with both, stresses protection of freedom by the laws and free obedience to them. As we move on to the very short chapter 38, we find that it reaches a higher level of excitement and that it, more than chapter 37, sets forth something spectacular. The life of the city is not to be thought of as basely utilitarian, but as providing a rich variety of things that are good in themselves—spiritual things like athletic contests, religious ceremonies, and beautiful buildings. Although the commerce of Athens was im-

---

[6] I shall use the term *Athenians* as a general term. There is a distinction between citizens and strangers, but the fact that the distinction makes very little difference in the life of Athens is one of the points Pericles stresses. A general term is needed, and the term *citizens* will not do.

portant for the necessities of life, Pericles does not stress its utilitarian value but speaks rather of the wealth of all the world; "the fruits of the labours of other lands" seem, in this context, to be more splendid than mere necessities, and their presence in Athens is due to her greatness and power.

The search for pattern may also reveal another dimension of the expansiveness just noted. Chapter 37 speaks of the political and social aspects of life within Athens herself. Chapter 38, as soon as it turns to athletics, religion, and art—with the expression "all the year round"—seems to carry our view beyond the limited sphere of internal politics and society; and it concludes, in turning to economics and commerce, by referring to the wealth of all the world.

It might be said, then, that in the first two substantial chapters we find a rather dramatic movement from a comparatively prosaic level to something like a sudden climax in Pericles' first grand picture of the splendor of Athens. But to exaggerate this dramatic progress would be misleading. An exaggeration could suggest that Pericles moves gradually and steadily toward a higher and higher level of eloquence. Such a "gradual" picture would fit an interpretation that finds the very first chapter almost disappointing in its cold disapproval of the tradition of the funeral speech and its almost insulting anticipations of audience reactions, and also finds the attitude toward ancestors, in chapter 36, faint praise, at best. What this exaggerated interpretation would obscure would be the definitely dramatic step that is taken at the very beginning of chapter 37. Political structure and social relationships may be less glamorous than athletic contests, religious ceremonies, and beautiful buildings, but as they are presented by Pericles, attention is drawn to the Athenian spirit that animates the political institutions and social manners. The first note that is struck, as Pericles turns to his main task, is the originality of the Athenian spirit, as manifested in its construction. We may learn from this that the spirit of Athens, which Pericles said he would speak of first, is expressed in a special way. It is not that he first speaks of it, and then speaks of the constitution and so forth. The constitution is indeed the first topic spoken of, but in the very way he speaks of it Pericles expresses the spirit of Athens. The spirit, then, is not one of several topics that are treated in sequential order, but rather a pervasive idea coloring everything that is said. If chapter 38 is correctly viewed as a sort of climax, it is a climax of the development of an idea about the Athenian spirit, which has dramatic force as soon as it is spoken of. Is not even its very first mention rather striking when, at the end of chapter 36, Pericles contrasts it—as something positively significant —with other topics he has no enthusiasm for: solemn words over the dead, ancestors, battles? Instead of a gradual rise in level of eloquence Pericles moves, so to speak, by waves. Even in the subdued tone of chapter 35 and 36 we can find something like a wave, which reaches its small climax at the mere mention of "the spirit in which we faced [the battles]," and the "greatness" to which we have risen.

Something like the same pattern (a wave with a still higher crest) can be found in the next pair of chapters, 39 and 40. This possibility should strike the reader if he looks at the beginning of chapter 40, with its famous "we are lovers of beauty without extravagance, and lovers of wisdom without unmanliness." The reader will surely feel that this reaches a higher level of eloquence than anything that precedes, and, at the very least, that it sets a tone for chapter 40 that makes the tone of 39 seem mild in contrast. But only in contrast. For the discussion of military training and of education in chapter 39, like the discussion of politics, society, and economics in 37, is permeated with the same spirit of Athenian freedom. Taken by themselves, however, military service, and education when thought of as subserving military service, are more utilitarian than the athletics, religion, art, and commerce that were contrasted, in chapter 38, with the activities of a "work-a-day city." They therefore seem to constitute a comparative decline from the crest of the wave reached at the end of chapter 38. But, as they ally themselves to the expansiveness that characterized the first reference to Athenian commerce (and they do this, because military service carries our view beyond the city itself, as do matters of foreign policy, which conclude chapter 40), so they prepare the way for the crest of the wave which opens chapter 41: "I claim that our city as a whole is an education to Greece."[7] In the two earlier "crests" Athens is referred to as splendid or glorious for the Athenians. At the beginning of chapter 41 its glory is a function of its supremacy in "all the world," a note that was first sounded at the end of chapter 37, but carried to new heights of eloquence in chapter 41, which finishes Pericles' setting forth of the Athenian spirit, constitution, and manners.

Chapters 37–41 stand in contrast to chapters 42–46, because the former have as their subject the city itself, and its life; the latter turn attention to the Athenians, who constitute the city and live its life. It is easy to subdivide the latter group. Chapter 44 turns at once to a new topic, mourning and comforting—not only a new topic, but one close to that which Pericles rejects in the opening chapter. The new topic introduced in chapter 44 is carried through chapter 45 in an orderly way: Pericles offers comfort to parents, brothers, children, and widows of the dead. The thematic unity of chapters 44 and 45 suggests that we may consider chapters 42 and 43 apart from them.

There are reasons why chapters 42 and 43 may be considered more substantial than the succeeding chapters, that is, closer than chapters 44–46 to Pericles' central concern. First, they are provided for in his original outline of his intentions, because in them he passes from the constitution and manners of Athens to the dead; the outline makes no provision for chapters 44–46. Second, the final group of chapters has functions that seem to balance the functions of chapters 35 and 36, which are plainly preliminary, not substantial. Chapters 35 and 36 refer first to the funeral ceremony itself and then to the ancestry of the fallen soldiers. Chapters 44–46 reverse this order, as well as the time perspective, in a balancing way: 44 and 45 speak of the posterity of the fallen soldiers, and

---

[7] Zimmern's translation was of course chosen for this book because of its excellence. The reader may also be interested in Crawley's fine version of this passage, in which Pericles speaks of Athens as "the school of Hellas" (Richard Crawley, trans., *The Complete Writings of Thucydides,* Modern Library ed. [New York, 1934]).

46 closes the speech with a final reference to the funeral ceremony. If we press this notion about substance we may be encouraged to say that chapters 37–41 are the main substance of the speech, that 42–43 are a reflection of that substance, and that 44–46 are a secondary reflection. This statement does fit the structure of the speech in some respects, and it fits our second summary statement better than the first. But I should be surprised if it seemed adequate to many readers, especially when applied to the second summary. For we should naturally ask why the various topics which "are made to support the main purpose" should be arranged as reflections of the main substance of the speech. We shall seek an answer by considering some details in chapters 42 and 43.

Pericles begins by explaining that he has "spent many words upon the city," in order to support his "praise of the dead by making clear to you what they have done." At first glance this statement does seem to support the idea (expressed in the first summary statement) that Pericles has "chanted the glories of the city" for the sake of praising the dead soldiers. His hearers might easily interpret him in this way, unless he did something to prevent such an interpretation. What does he do? First, he never lets the thought of the splendor of Athens fade in his listeners' minds. Second, he works strenuously and ingeniously to identify the listeners with the dead, as servants of Athens. Even as he turns to praise the dead, he praises them for what they have done, for Athens; and it is they "and their like"—included in the audience—who have arrayed her. The dead and the survivors are alike because their glory is the reflected glory of Athens. Pericles finds an ingenious way of emphasizing this idea by turning to those of the Athenian dead whose lives, aside from their "last brave hour of devotion," were disgraceful rather than honorable: these "did the city more service as soldiers than they did her harm in private life."

Chapter 43 is especially interesting, both in itself and because of its position in the speech as a whole. In itself it is most striking because it contains Pericles' most brilliant expression of the glory of the Athenian spirit: "let us draw strength . . . from the busy spectacle of our great city's life as we have it before us day by day, falling in love with her as we see her . . ." But the very eloquence of this expression can present a problem about its position in the speech. Suppose that our interpretation favors the second summary statement rather than the first; then chapter 43, which concludes Pericles' remarks about the dead, is the last part of the main substance of the speech (if chapters 44–46 provide, along with the initial two chapters, a sort of framework). It, along with chapter 42, speaks of the dead, which Pericles has said would be his final topic. But our second statement suggests that the remarks about the dead are not the main thing; and Pericles' own words (in chapters 35 and 36) support this interpretation. Why then does chapter 43 contain the most eloquent of all Pericles' expressions of the glory of the Athenian spirit? Perhaps the first summary statement is the better one, after all. Pericles has all along had as his main purpose the epideictic one of praising the fallen soldiers—he has praised the city to support his praise for the dead.

The latter interpretation may gain support if we consider the climactic sentence about "the busy spectacle of our great city's life," not only in itself, but also in its immediate context. It can be easily fitted into the structure suggested by the wave metaphor. Pericles has finished chapter 42 on a very high level of eloquence in speaking of the courageous deaths of the soldiers as "the climax of their lives." He assumes that his hearers will, to some extent at least, admire this courage simply as courage. Ordinary courage is admirable enough, but it falls far short of the courage that can be inspired in the Athenians by the splendor of their city. Ordinary courage can be inspired by "twice-told arguments—how fair and noble a thing it is to show courage in battle." But "let us draw strength," he says, "from the busy spectacle of our great city's life."

Then can the interpretation suggested by the second summary statement be held only at the cost of regarding the speech's most eloquent sentence as a kind of anticlimax? We have already noted that the spirit of Athens can be taken to be Pericles' main theme and that it is not one of several topics treated in sequential order but a pervasive idea that colors everything that is said. As such it is independent of the order of other topics. The topic which, for Pericles, is comparatively unimportant, the dead, is not a topic he can avoid; the occasion is, after all, a funeral ceremony. He can so speak of the dead, however, that when he praises them he praises the spirit of the city even more. This he achieves in a most remarkable way. He elevates the ideal of the city, wave by wave, from chapter 37 through chapter 41. He then turns, as he has said he would, to the dead. But the dead are not allowed to capture the main interest of the audience. Even as he praises what is most praiseworthy about fallen soldiers—their honor, devotion, and courage—he brings forward once more the image of the glory of Athens, and it is not inappropriate for that image to shine more brilliantly here than before.

(Many theories of art have placed rhetoric and poetics very close to each other. The point that has just been discussed brings out one reason why this is so. An orator like Pericles could not succeed with the very difficult problem we have just considered unless he had extraordinary poetic ability—this oration which illustrates one of the closest bonds between rhetoric and poetry shows his ability to hit upon striking figures of speech, figures that not only express what he means but express it with just the necessary vividness of feeling.)

We still prefer, then, an interpretation along the lines of the second summary statement. This view, as it has developed, gives a special function to Pericles' main theme, the spirit of Athens, a function which it performs throughout the speech—not just at one point. The suggested interpretation can be supported by the use of distinctions that have been worked out in classical theories of rhetoric. Suppose that we ask whether the speech is epideictic or deliberative. Our two summary statements both tend to regard it as epideictic. According to the first statement it is a speech in praise of the dead; according to the second, it praises the city. Which statement is more favorable to interpreting the speech as deliberative? That would depend on what Pericles' deliberative purpose might be. What else could it be than the purpose of in-

spiring the living Athenians to devote themselves to the utmost
to the Athenian ideal? Such a deliberative purpose is served by the
mounting eloquence of Pericles' expression of the Athenian spirit.
The ceremonial necessity of speaking of the dead might actually
blunt that purpose, except for Pericles' ability to make the city
shine most brightly at the very point in his speech when he praises
the dead.

Classical theories suggest that a deliberative speech would give
strong emphasis to argument. So, as I mentioned above, Aristotle
distinguishes three elements in rhetoric: the speaker, the speech,
and the audience. The essential element of the speech is its argument, and arguments have structures that distinguish them from
the characters of the men who speak, and from the passions of the
men who listen. We tend to think of the structure of an argument
as a logical structure, but we should also expect that logical structure in rhetoric is not the same as in science or philosophy. We shall
say more about the differences later.[8] For the present let it suffice
that there are situations in which the praise of something can
be like an argument persuading men to act in a certain way.
Pericles faced such a situation, and the most persuasive argument
he could use was the expression of ideals capable of inspiring new
strength in the Athenians for the ordeals that lay ahead.

I have been developing the first of the two points mentioned
above (p. 162), that Pericles never lets the thought of the splendor
of Athens fade in his listeners' minds. I hope the reader is per-
suaded that the sentence about the busy spectacle of our great
city's life is in no way an anticlimax. But I fear that, after its eloquence has been so much insisted on, it will indeed seem anticlimactic to take up the second point, about the identification of the
dead with the survivors. In order to present a meaningful identification, what is to be identified must also be clearly distinguished.
The distinction is expressly made by Pericles. Just as, at the end of
chapter 41 he distinguishes between "the city" and "the men . . .

---

[8] Pp. 169–70, below.

who died a soldier's death," he distinguishes at the beginning of chapter 43 between "the men who lie here," and "we survivors" (or "you survivors," as it might be translated). We have seen that the first distinction, between the city and the men, tended to be obliterated, because the men were to be honored for what they had done for the city. At the point where this is done, Pericles uses the pronoun *we* to produce a similar effect in obliterating the distinction between the dead and the survivors. At the beginning of chapter 42 it is what "we have . . . at stake" that matters—the same thing was at stake for the dead which is at stake for the living. The identification of the dead with the survivors is given an eloquent expression, after the remark about "the busy spectacle of our great city's life"; the expression is beautiful enough to prevent the remark from being anticlimactic, even at the late point where it appears, so soon after "the busy spectacle." He expresses the idea of identification by saying that the dead have a home not in the earth where their bones will be laid, but in the minds of men; and that their story is not a story told and finished, but a story still going on, "woven into the stuff of other men's lives." The dead and the living are united, because what gives them their significance and value, in each case, is the spirit of Athens which they have breathed together and—in a sense—still share.

Pericles' reference to "the sepulchre of famous men" is the first explicit reference to funeral ceremonies since chapter 35. It should now be clear why he disapproved of the custom of speaking solemn words over the dead. "Solemn" words, in the tradition of funeral ceremonies, would emphasize the deadness of the fallen soldiers; Pericles has emphasized the vitality of the Athenian spirit. Identifying the dead with that vital spirit, Pericles has made his hearers' minds dwell not on the idea that the fallen soldiers are dead but on the glorious contribution they made, "at the climax of their lives," to "our great city's life." The reference to "the sepulchre of famous men" also provides a transition to the subjects of the remaining chapters, mourning and comfort.

If chapters 44–46 were not preceded by chapters 37–43 it might seem that Pericles offers only cold comfort to the bereaved. The force of his "therefore" (in "Therefore I do not mourn") should be clear by now, however, and it is interesting to see that he treats the bereaved, just as he has treated the survivors generally, primarily as fellow Athenians with the dead. (It is in this sense that the treatment of survivors, and then of bereaved relatives, can be considered a reflection and a secondary reflection, respectively, of the main substance of the speech.) The family relationship is played down in this chapter and considered to be secondary in importance to the relationship of fellow Athenians. Parents who are still able to bear children must draw courage from that capability, because through it they can continue to serve the city as they have already served her, as parents. Other parents must struggle against the reminder of loss brought to them by the sight of the children of others and must seek consolation in the thought of the glory the dead have won defending Athens. The "comfort" offered to brothers, children, and widows may be hard for a twentieth-century American audience to sympathize with; but even that would harmonize with the rest of the speech for anyone who could fully accept the ideal of citizenship expressed by Pericles.

The discussion has thus far tried to hold closely to what can be found in the text of the speech itself. We have to some extent made use of theoretical ideas concerning such distinctions as that between epideictic and deliberative rhetoric; and we have distinguished the argument of the speech from other features. The reader who focuses his attention on the rhetorical aspects of literature should ask himself how the speaker is characterized, and what effect his character produces. He should also ask how the feelings of the audience help to account for details of the text. In this particular speech, at least on a comparatively elementary level of analysis, consideration of the character of the speaker is not very rewarding; this is because Pericles so carefully refrains from giving himself any character except that of an Athenian, and in this character he prefers not to seem different from the fallen soldiers or the survivors. On a more complicated level of analysis there is plenty of rewarding work the reader could do, such as a study of the speaker's style; in his style Pericles, as presented by

Thucydides, is not just any Athenian. But an analysis of style should be undertaken only when the reader understands the original language.

Just as the speaker may take on a character by virtue of the remarks he makes, so the audience can be in a sense "made" by the speech. Some speeches may make more or less explicit appeals to interests and attitudes that one possible audience would have, as opposed to some other possible audience. Sometimes, even though only one possible audience is in the speaker's mind, he may so appeal to his listeners as to get them to think of themselves in a way favorable to the speaker's words. Pericles does this, for he wants the audience to think of itself as filled with the spirit which is the main subject of his eulogy. The extent to which it was actually filled with that spirit could be the subject of historical debate. We have here an indication of something the reader should take a different attitude toward, when his interest is in rhetoric, than he would when his interest is in history. Alfred Zimmern, the translator of Pericles' speech, is a good historian as well as a good translator. He appends footnotes to his translation which show that he is looking at the speech from a point of view more of history than rhetoric. For example, he would like to correct Pericles when he speaks, in chapter 36, of "the city's complete independence," and of the manner in which the Athenians have withstood "the warfare of barbarian or Greek at home." But the rhetorical point that Zimmern misses is that Pericles is presenting a picture he knows his audience wants to believe. Pericles offers no proof of some of his statements precisely because the audience needs no proof. If there are statements which cannot be proved (how can you prove what is just not so?), the audience, if it felt flattered by them, would not think of asking for proof. It might just prefer to believe. An inaccurate or untrue statement may be a blemish in a historical writing, but it need not be a blemish from a rhetorical point of view. Consider Pericles' remarks as they affect a twentieth-century audience, rather than his actual audience. It may not matter much to us that the Athenians fell short of Pericles' ideal, whereas the ideal itself, as expressed by him, is capable of moving us deeply.

Although the preceding paragraph deals with the audience, its remarks bear also on the difference between what we may call strict logic and rhetorical logic. In science and philosophy it is expected that demonstrative arguments will have no real gaps in them. If the writer does not prove each logically necessary premise, he nevertheless assumes that his readers (who may require special knowledge if they are to understand him) know how to prove them.

In rhetorical works this is not so, for two reasons. First, even a particular audience is "general" in the sense that it shares no special knowledge (we are not thinking of an audience of physicists or lawyers, considering a speech on physics or law). So the speaker cannot in such cases prove certain things, because the audience would not be able to follow the proof.

Second, the audience may share beliefs which are—at least in the present state of knowledge—incapable of being proved. It would be improper for a scientist or philosopher to rest his arguments on such beliefs, except in a hypothetical way. If it were improper for the orator to do so (and it is not improper), the potentialities of rhetoric would be severely limited. Audiences do hold certain beliefs. Some of these beliefs are unshakable. Others can be modified, but even if the orator undertakes to modify them he must begin by recognizing that the audience holds them. If the orator wants to persuade his audience (and he may be morally obligated to do his best, even where the chances are slim) he must know what his audience believes. He must try to exploit these beliefs rhetorically; and this may mean that their truth or falsity does not at the moment matter.

The difference between strict and rhetorical logic gives us another way of distinguishing essentially rhetorical pieces from others which are rhetorical only in a secondary sense. To the extent that the argument of a work rests on premises that are not proved, that argument is rhetorical. What constitutes a proof is often, of course, very difficult to say.[9] Accordingly, the line between the two kinds of logic is not sharp. Scientists and philosophers have their beliefs too, as well as their knowledge, and they cannot always be sure which is which. How often can anyone be sure that a given point has been demonstrated?

We may summarize this discussion of the peculiarities of rhetorical argument by saying that if a proposition is necessary for that argument the question is not whether the proposition is true but whether the audience believes, or can be made to believe, that it is true.

Some students of literature have conceived of rhetoric so broadly as to regard everything an author does in order to produce a certain effect upon his readers as rhetorical in purpose. Such a view tends to obscure the literary importance of what I have regarded as non-rhetorical features. How can the scope of rhetorical analysis be limited so as to prevent the neglect of other useful modes of analysis?

One way of keeping rhetorical analysis within bounds may be mentioned. Any characteristics that a piece of drama, fiction, history, or philosophy may have which seem calculated to affect, not the substance of what is said (e.g., the plot in drama or fiction, what happened in history, or what is inquired into in philosophy), but the readers' attitude toward that substance, may be regarded as rhetorical. It is much easier to say this than to follow it intelligently. The more experience one has in reading, the more one is impressed with the difficulty of making, in any concrete way, the sort of distinction here called for. Nevertheless the effort to apply

---

[9] It is not meant here that a premise is not proved unless the proof is actually stated in the work in question. There are statements whose proofs are readily available, either for a general audience or for an audience with special knowledge. The recognition of authority can also bridge the gap between the two kinds of audience. That is, a general audience can recognize a person of special competence and regard him as an authority in his field. His testimony can be correctly regarded as proved, even when the proof is not given (and there would be no point in giving it to an audience incapable of following it). But on the question of authority we are in a kind of no man's land between strict and rhetorical argument.

the distinction to the particular works we read will reveal important things about them, even if we finally decide that the distinction should not be applied. In our efforts to apply it we may ask what the author does to influence the reader to approve or disapprove of a character, an event, an idea, an argument; to pass judgment upon any of these; or to move toward taking action in some definite direction. If, after we have duly considered these questions, we decide that the author does not allow what he writes to be determined by any purpose other than influencing the reader in one of these ways, then we may regard that work as essentially rhetorical, whether it is a short speech, a three-volume novel, or a system of philosophy.

If it be thought that one mark of an essentially rhetorical work is its being addressed to a very limited audience, the thought can be misleading. It arises from the fact that works that have no universal appeal do seem to be rhetorical, and it is encouraged by the idea that an effect upon a particular audience is an important consideration in rhetoric, but not in history, poetry, or philosophy. But what we call great pieces of rhetoric do appeal to universal audiences—Pericles' speech is a good case in point. They have not, by virtue of their universal appeal, become works of history or philosophy, because their use of evidence and argument is still rhetorical.

The remaining paragraphs are intended as concluding remarks not only for this chapter on rhetoric, but for the book as a whole. Throughout, the effort has been to focus attention upon what can be found in the texts themselves. This is where the first and last emphases should be placed in reading. One's reading can be enriched, however, if reference is also made to materials outside the texts we are reading.

There are two ways in which reading, which basically involves a reader and a book can be broadened. The reader's approach can be broadened by expanding what he brings to his reading. A logical first step is to join with other readers and to discuss the books one reads. We all do tend to do this. If we like a book we want to discuss it with someone else. If we are trying to develop our reading abilities systematically, it follows that this first step should be taken systematically. Reading programs should be undertaken with other persons (including those with different points of view). The better the other readers, the better for us. We should not stop with readers who are physically available to us. What other good readers have written about the books we read should eventually be explored by anyone who wants the richest experience in reading.

The second way to broaden one's reading is to bring more into it from the side of the book. To do this is not altogether different from following the first mode, just discussed; for by means of it more on "the side of the book" will inevitably be brought in. The second mode can be illustrated with reference to Pericles' speech. As we have it, it is handed to us by Thucydides, who competent authorities think may have written it about thirty years after Pericles died. Thucydides himself tells us that the speeches he presents are not necessarily the actual words spoken on the particular occasion. What are we to make of this? We may simply take the speech (as thus far we have taken it) as a piece of writing; and we may analyze it without reference to its context. But to consider it in its context is appropriate; we may ask what is the significance of the fact that it was written by Thucydides thirty years after Pericles spoke it. One obvious difference is that Thucydides' actual audience could not have been the same as Pericles' actual audience. Everything we may know about the Peloponnesian War can help us interpret this. And, if we read the rest of Thucydides' history, we may learn much that is useful to a thorough understanding of the speech.

We may learn from Thucydides that the speech was given after the first year of the war. At that time the Athenians had no strong reason to be pessimistic about the outcome of the war. Much that Thucydides tells us encourages us to believe that they shared the spirit so well expressed in the speech—certainly that they shared it more fully then than they did later, especially after the war's disastrous end (at the time when Thucydides may have written it). He tells us too that it was given before the great plague struck

Athens; and there is good reason to think Thucydides believed that the spirit of Athens was never the same after the plague. It is strongly possible that Thucydides wrote his history with definite rhetorical aims; if he did so his version of Pericles' speech could well have been colored by those aims; and Thucydides' aims must have been different from those of Pericles himself, since the task and the audience before Pericles were very different.

If a complete reading of Thucydides can change a reader's understanding of Pericles' speech (and the change would surely be one of enrichment and greater adequacy), a greater understanding of the civilization of ancient Greece can make further contributions.[10] The reading of other literature written by the ancient Greeks themselves, as well as the study of secondary works by men who have read the original works thoughtfully, is essential if the reader is to achieve thorough understanding. In other words, books are not to be read in isolation from one another. The understanding of one book should contribute to the illumination of another.

The development of the capacity for intelligent reading does not stop with reading alone. The ultimate significance of good reading should lie in its becoming a part of one's thinking, of one's life. Reading can even be dangerous, if it is allowed to control the way we think; but it can be invaluable to the extent that it provokes thought. With reference to philosophy Kant has expressed this well in his distinction between historical and rational knowledge.[11] Rhetorical literature (and poetry and history also) can stimulate thought by means of the conflicts that may arise in the reader's mind as he studies one of its great examples, such as Pericles' *Funeral Oration*. One can imagine Thucydides' immediate audience wondering, amid the ruins of Athens, what happened to the spirit and the ideal Pericles had spoken of. Did the war turn out disastrously for Athens because Pericles' ideal was not in fact

---

[10] Zimmern's *Greek Commonwealth* (see note 1 above) is one book that can be of great help and interest.

[11] Immanuel Kant, *Critique of Pure Reason*, trans. N. K. Smith (London: Macmillan & Co., 1963), p. 655.

shared by his audience, or because he misconceived it? Such questions can be meaningful for us too, 2,500 years later (and Thucydides said he was writing his history "as a possession for all time"). We might also ask: Was the Athenian devotion to the ideal imperfect? Was it shattered by the opposition of a stronger ideal, or a more dedicated people?[12] Is the ideal one that we should dedicate ourselves to today? Is the ideal itself defective? Or are we capable of dedication to it? The reader must consider all such questions with his own mental resources. Neither Pericles nor Thucydides answers them for him; he must stop reading and start thinking on his own.

---

[12] An alert reader will have noticed that the present analysis of Pericles' speech pays no attention to his allusions to the Spartan enemies of Athens. The allusions are indeed there, and a thorough analysis would have to say something about them. The present analysis does not pretend to be anything more than introductory, and will have succeeded in its purpose if it leads the reader to carry out rhetorical analyses that improve his own understanding.

Appendix I

John Dewey, "Habits as Social Functions"

[1] Habits may be profitably compared to physiological functions, like breathing, digesting. The latter are, to be sure, involuntary, while habits are acquired. But important as is this difference for many purposes it should not conceal the fact that habits are like functions in many respects, and especially in requiring the cooperation of organism and environment. Breathing is an affair of the air as truly as of the lungs; digesting an affair of food as truly as of tissues of stomach. Seeing involves light just as certainly as it does the eye and optic nerve. Walking implicates the ground as well as the legs; speech demands physical air and human companionship and audience as well as vocal organs. We may shift from the biological to the mathematical use of the word function, and say that natural operations like breathing and digesting, acquired ones like speech and honesty, are functions of the surroundings as truly as of a person. They are things done *by* the environment by means of organic structures or acquired dispositions. The same air that under certain conditions ruffles the pool or wrecks buildings, under other conditions purifies the blood and conveys thought. The outcome depends upon what air acts upon. The social environment acts through native impulses and speech and moral habitudes manifest themselves. There are specific good

reasons for the usual attribution of acts to the person from whom they immediately proceed. But to convert this special reference into a belief of exclusive ownership is as misleading as to suppose that breathing and digesting are complete within the human body. To get a rational basis for moral discussion we must begin with recognizing that functions and habits are ways of using and incorporating the environment in which the latter has its say as surely as the former.

[2] We may borrow words from a context less technical than that of biology, and convey the same idea by saying that habits are arts. They involve skill of sensory and motor organs, cunning or craft, and objective materials. They assimilate objective energies, and eventuate in command of environment. They require order, discipline, and manifest technique. They have a beginning, middle and end. Each stage marks progress in dealing with materials and tools, advance in converting material to active use. We should laugh at any one who said that he was master of stone working, but that the art was cooped up within himself and in no wise dependent upon support from objects and assistance from tools.

[3] In morals we are however quite accustomed to such a fatuity. Moral dispositions are thought of as belonging exclusively to a self. The self is thereby isolated from natural and social surroundings. A whole school of morals flourishes upon capital drawn from restricting morals to character and then separating character from conduct, motives from actual deeds. Recognition of the analogy of moral action with functions and arts uproots the causes which have made morals subjective and "individualistic." It brings morals to earth, and if they still aspire to heaven it is to the heavens *of* the earth, and not to another world. Honesty, chastity, malice, peevishness, courage, triviality, industry, irresponsibility are not private possessions of a person. They are working adaptations of personal capacities with environing forces. All virtues and vices are habits which incorporate objective forces. They are interactions of elements contributed by the make-up of an individual with elements supplied by the out-door world. They can be studied as objectively

as physiological functions, and they can be modified by change of either personal or social elements.

[4] If an individual were alone in the world, he would form his habits (assuming the impossible, namely, that he would be able to form them) in a moral vacuum. They would belong to him alone, or to him only in reference to physical forces. Responsibility and virtue would be his alone. But since habits involve the support of environing conditions, a society or some specific group of fellow-men, is always accessory before and after the fact. Some activity proceeds from a man; then it sets up reactions in the surroundings. Others approve, disapprove, protest, encourage, share and resist. Even letting a man alone is a definite response. Envy, admiration and imitation are complicities. Neutrality is non-existent. Conduct is always shared; this is the difference between it and a physiological process. It is not an ethical "ought" that conduct *should* be social. It *is* social, whether bad or good.

[5] Washing one's hands of the guilt of others is a way of sharing guilt so far as it encourages in others a vicious way of action. Non-resistance to evil which takes the form of paying no attention to it is a way of promoting it. The desire of an individual to keep his own conscience stainless by standing aloof from badness may be a sure means of causing evil and thus of creating personal responsibility for it. Yet there are circumstances in which passive resistance may be the most effective form of nullification of wrong action, or in which heaping coals of fire on the evil-doer may be the most effective way of transforming conduct. To sentimentalize over a criminal—to "forgive" because of a glow of feeling—is to incur liability for production of criminals. But to suppose that infliction of retributive suffering suffices, without reference to concrete consequences, is to leave untouched old causes of criminality and to create new ones by fostering revenge and brutality. The abstract theory of justice which demands the "vindication" of law irrespective of instruction and reform of the wrong-doer is as much a refusal to recognize responsibility as is the sentimental gush which makes a suffering victim out of a criminal.

[6] Courses of action which put the blame exclusively on a person as if his evil will were the sole cause of wrong-doing and those which condone offense on account of the share of social conditions in producing bad disposition, are equally ways of making an unreal separation of man from his surroundings, mind from the world. Causes for an act always exist, but causes are not excuses. Questions of causation are physical, not moral except when they concern future consequences. It is as causes of future actions that excuses and accusations alike must be considered. At present we give way to resentful passion, and then "rationalize" our surrender by calling it a vindication of justice. Our entire tradition regarding punitive justice tends to prevent recognition of social partnership in producing crime; it falls in with a belief in metaphysical free-will. By killing an evil-doer or shutting him up behind stone walls, we are enabled to forget both him and our part in creating him. Society excuses itself by laying the blame on the criminal; he retorts by putting the blame on bad early surroundings, the temptations of others, lack of opportunities, and the persecutions of officers of the law. Both are right, except in the wholesale character of their recriminations. But the effect on both sides is to throw the whole matter back into antecedent causation, a method which refuses to bring the matter to truly moral judgment. For morals has to do with acts still within our control, acts still to be performed. No amount of guilt on the part of the evil-doer absolves us from responsibility for the consequences upon him and others of our way of treating him, or from our continuing responsibility for the conditions under which persons develop perverse habits.

[7] We need to discriminate between the physical and the moral question. The former concerns what *has* happened, and how it happened. To consider this question is indispensable to morals. Without an answer to it we cannot tell what forces are at work nor how to direct our actions so as to improve conditions. Until we know the conditions which have helped form the characters we approve and disapprove, our efforts to create the one and do away with the other will be blind and halting. But the moral issue concerns the future. It is prospective. To content ourselves with pro-

nouncing judgments of merit and demerit without reference to the fact that our judgments are themselves facts which have consequences and that their value depends upon *their* consequences, is complacently to dodge the moral issue, perhaps even to indulge ourselves in pleasurable passion just as the person we condemn once indulged himself. The moral problem is that of modifying the factors which now influence future results. To change the working character or will of another we have to alter objective conditions which enter into his habits. Our own schemes of judgment, of assigning blame and praise, of awarding punishment and honor, are part of these conditions.

[8] In practical life, there are many recognitions of the part played by social factors in generating personal traits. One of them is our habit of making social classifications. We attribute distinctive characteristics to rich and poor, slum-dweller and captain of industry, rustic and suburbanite, officials, politicians, professors, to members of races, sets and parties. These judgments are usually too coarse to be of much use. But they show our practical awareness that personal traits are functions of social situations. When we generalize this perception and act upon it intelligently we are committed by it to recognize that we change character from worse to better only by changing conditions—among which, once more, are our own ways of dealing with the one we judge. We cannot change habit directly: that notion is magic. But we can change it indirectly by modifying conditions, by an intelligent selecting and weighting of the objects which engage attention and which influence the fulfillment of desires.

[9] A savage can travel after a fashion in a jungle. Civilized activity is too complex to be carried on without smoothed roads. It requires signals and junction points; traffic authorities and means of easy and rapid transportation. It demands a congenial, antecedently prepared environment. Without it, civilization would relapse into barbarism in spite of the best of subjective intention and internal good disposition. The eternal dignity of labor and art lies in their effecting that permanent reshaping of environment which is the substantial foundation of future security and progress. In-

dividuals flourish and wither away like the grass of the fields. But the fruits of their work endure and make possible the development of further activities having fuller significance. It is of grace not of ourselves that we lead civilized lives. There is sound sense in the old pagan notion that gratitude is the root of all virtue. Loyalty to whatever in the established environment makes a life of excellence possible is the beginning of all progress. The best we can accomplish for posterity is to transmit unimpaired and with some increment of meaning the environment that makes it possible to maintain the habits of decent and refined life. Our individual habits are links in forming the endless chain of humanity. Their significance depends upon the environment inherited from our forerunners, and it is enhanced as we foresee the fruits of our labors in the world in which our successors live.

[10] For however much has been done, there always remains more to do. We can retain and transmit our own heritage only by constant remaking of our own environment. Piety to the past is not for its own sake nor for the sake of the past, but for the sake of a present so secure and enriched that it will create a yet better future. Individuals with their exhortations, their preachings and scoldings, their inner aspirations and sentiments have disappeared, but their habits endure, because these habits incorporate objective conditions in themselves. So will it be with *our* activities. We may desire abolition of war, industrial justice, greater equality of opportunity for all. But no amount of preaching good will or the golden rule or cultivation of sentiments of love and equity will accomplish the results. There must be change in objective arrangements and institutions. We must work on the environment not merely on the hearts of men. To think otherwise is to suppose that flowers can be raised in a desert or motor cars run in a jungle. Both things can happen and without a miracle. But only by first changing the jungle and desert.

[11] Yet the distinctively personal or subjective factors in habit count. Taste for flowers may be the initial step in building reservoirs and irrigation canals. The stimulation of desire and effort is one preliminary in the change of surroundings. While personal

exhortation, advice and instruction is a feeble stimulus compared with that which steadily proceeds from the impersonal forces and depersonalized habitudes of the environment, yet they may start the latter going. Taste, appreciation and effort always spring from some accomplished objective situation. They have objective support; they represent the liberation of something formerly accomplished so that it is useful in further operation. A genuine appreciation of the beauty of flowers is not generated within a self-enclosed consciousness. It reflects a world in which beautiful flowers have already grown and been enjoyed. Taste and desire represent a prior objective fact recurring in action to secure perpetuation and extension. Desire for flowers comes after actual enjoyment of flowers. But it comes before the work that makes the desert blossom, it comes before *cultivation* of plants. Every ideal is preceded by an actuality; but the ideal is more than a repetition in inner image of the actual. It projects in securer and wider and fuller form some good which has been previously experienced in a precarious, accidental, fleeting way.

Appendix II

Pericles' Funeral Oration

(34) In the same winter, following the law of their fathers, the Athenians held the first public funeral of those who had fallen in the war. The ceremony is as follows. The bones of the dead are exposed on a covered platform for three days, during which any one may place his personal offerings at their side. On the third day they are laid in ten coffins of cypress wood, one for each tribe, every man's bones in the coffin of his tribe; these are put on carriages and driven to the grave. One empty bed covered with a winding sheet is also borne for the missing whose bodies were not recovered for burning. All who so desire, whether citizens or strangers, may join in the procession, and the women folk of the dead are at the graveside bewailing them. The interment takes place in the State burial ground, which is situated in the most beautiful suburb of the city. All Athenians who have died in war lie buried there, except those who fell at Marathon; their valour was adjudged so conspicuous that the funeral was held on the field of battle. When the coffins have been laid in the earth some speaker elected by the city for his wisdom and public estimation delivers an appropriate eulogy; after this the gathering disperses. This is the customary ceremonial, and it was adhered to throughout the war whenever occasion arose. It was at the funeral of this first group of fallen that Pericles the son of Xanthippus was elected to speak. When the moment came, he stepped forward from the graveside on to a high platform made for the occasion, so that his voice might carry as far as possible over the crowd, and spoke as follows:

Reprinted from Alfred Zimmern, *The Greek Commonwealth* (5th ed.; London: Oxford University Press, 1931), by permission of the Clarendon Press, Oxford.

(35) Most of those who have stood in this place before me have commended the institution of this closing address. It is good, they have felt, that solemn words should be spoken over our fallen soldiers. I do not share this feeling. Acts deserve acts, not words, in their honour, and to me a burial at the State's charges, such as you see before you, would have appeared sufficient. Our sense of the deserts of a number of our fellow-citizens should not depend upon the felicity of one man's speech. Moreover, it is very hard for a speaker to be appropriate when many of his hearers will scarce believe that he is truthful. For those who have known and loved the dead may think his words scant justice to the memories they would hear honoured: while those who do not know will occasionally, from jealousy suspect me of overstatement when they hear of any feat beyond their own powers. For it is only human for men not to bear praise of others beyond the point at which they still feel that they can rival their exploits. Transgress that boundary and they are jealous and distrustful. But since the wisdom of our ancestors enacted this law I too must submit and try to suit as best I can the wishes and feelings of every member of this gathering.

(36) My first words shall be for our ancestors; for it is both just to them and seemly that on an occasion such as this our tribute of memory should be paid them. For, dwelling always in this country, generation after generation in unchanging and unbroken succession, they have handed it down to us free by their exertions. So they are worthy of our praises; and still more so are our fathers. For they enlarged the ancestral patrimony by the Empire which we hold to-day and delivered it, not without labour, into the hands of our own generation; while it is we ourselves, those of us who are now in middle life, who consolidated our power throughout the greater part of the Empire and secured the city's complete independence both in war and peace. Of the battles which we and our fathers fought, whether in the winning of our power abroad or in bravely withstanding the warfare of barbarian or Greek at home, I do not wish to say more: they are too familiar to you all. I wish rather to set forth the spirit in which we faced them, and the constitution and manners with which we rose to greatness, and to pass from them to the dead; for I think it not unfitting that these

things should be called to mind at to-day's solemnity, and expedient too that the whole gathering of citizens and strangers should listen to them.

(37) For our government is not copied from those of our neighbours: we are an example to them rather than they to us. Our constitution is named a democracy, because it is in the hands not of the few but of the many. But our laws secure equal justice for all in their private disputes, and our public opinion welcomes and honours talent in every branch of achievement, not for any sectional reason but on grounds of excellence alone. And as we give free play to all in our public life, so we carry the same spirit into our daily relations with one another. We have no black looks or angry words for our neighbour if he enjoys himself in his own way, and we abstain from the little acts of churlishness which, though they leave no mark, yet cause annoyance to whoso notes them. Open and friendly in our private intercourse, in our public acts we keep strictly within the control of law. We acknowledge the restraint of reverence; we are obedient to whomsoever is set in authority, and to the laws, more especially to those which offer protection to the oppressed and those unwritten ordinances whose transgression brings admitted shame. (38) Yet ours is no work-a-day city only. No other provides so many recreations for the spirit—contests and sacrifices all the year round, and beauty in our public buildings to cheer the heart and delight the eye day by day. Moreover, the city is so large and powerful that all the wealth of all the world flows in to her, so that our own Attic products seem no more homelike to us than the fruits of the labours of other nations.

(39) Our military training too is different from our opponents'. The gates of our city are flung open to the world. We practise no periodical deportations, nor do we prevent our visitors from observing or discovering what an enemy might usefully apply to his own purposes. For our trust is not in the devices of material equipment, but in our own good spirits for battle.

So too with education. They toil from early boyhood in a laborious pursuit after courage, while we, free to live and wander as we please, march out none the less to face the self-same dangers.

Here is the proof of my words. When the Spartans advance into our country, they do not come alone but with all their allies; but when we invade our neighbours we have little difficulty as a rule, even on foreign soil, in defeating men who are fighting for their own homes. Moreover, no enemy has ever met us in full strength, for we have our navy to attend to, and our soldiers are sent on service to many scattered possessions; but if they chance to encounter some portion of our forces and defeat a few of us, they boast that they have driven back our whole army, or, if they are defeated, that the victors were in full strength. Indeed, if we choose to face danger with an easy mind rather than after a rigorous training, and to trust rather in native manliness than in state-made courage, the advantage lies with us; for we are spared all the weariness of practising for future hardships, and when we find ourselves amongst them we are as brave as our plodding rivals. Here as elsewhere, then, the city sets an example which is deserving of admiration. (40) We are lovers of beauty without extravagance, and lovers of wisdom without unmanliness. Wealth to us is not mere material for vainglory but an opportunity for achievement; and poverty we think it no disgrace to acknowledge but a real degradation to make no effort to overcome. Our citizens attend both to public and private duties, and do not allow absorption in their own various affairs to interfere with their knowledge of the city's. We differ from other states in regarding the man who holds aloof from public life not as 'quiet' but as useless; we decide or debate, carefully and in person, all matters of policy, holding, not that words and deeds go ill together, but that acts are foredoomed to failure when undertaken undiscussed. For we are noted for being at once most adventurous in action and most reflective beforehand. Other men are bold in ignorance, while reflection will stop their onset. But the bravest are surely those who have the clearest vision of what is before them, glory and danger alike, and yet notwithstanding go out to meet it. In doing good, too, we are the exact opposite of the rest of mankind. We secure our friends not by accepting favours but by doing them. And so we are naturally more firm in our attachments: for we are anxious, as creditors, to cement by kind offices our relation towards our friends. If they do not respond with the same warmness it is because they feel that their services will not be given spontaneously but only as the repayment of a debt. We are alone among mankind in doing men benefits, not on calculations of self-interest, but in the fearless confidence of freedom. (41) In a word I claim that our city as a whole is an education to Greece, and that her members yield to none, man by man, for independence of spirit, many-sidedness of attainment, and complete self-reliance in limbs and brain.

That this is no vainglorious phrase but actual fact the supremacy which our manners have won us itself bears testimony. No other city of the present day goes out to her ordeal greater than ever men dreamed; no other is so powerful that the invader feels no bitterness when he suffers at her hands, and her subjects no shame at the indignity of their dependence. Great indeed are the symbols and witnesses of our supremacy, at which posterity, as all mankind to-day, will be astonished. We need no Homer or other man of words to praise us; for such give pleasure for a moment, but the truth will put to shame their imaginings of our deeds. For our pioneers have forced a way into every sea and every land, establishing among all mankind, in punishment or beneficence, eternal memorials of their settlement.

Such then is the city for whom, lest they should lose her, the men whom we celebrate died a soldier's death: and it is but natural that all of us, who survive them, should wish to spend ourselves in her service. (42) That, indeed, is why I have spent many words upon the city. I wished to show that we have more at stake than men who have no such inheritance, and to support my praise of the dead by making clear to you what they have done. For if I have chanted the glories of the city it was these men and their like who set hand to array her. With them, as with few among Greeks, words cannot magnify the deeds that they have done. Such an end as we have here seems indeed to show us what a good life is, from its first signs of power to its final consummation. For even where life's previous record showed faults and failures it is just to weigh the last brave hour of devotion against them all. There they wiped out evil with good and did the city more service as soldiers than they did her harm in private life. There no hearts grew faint because they loved riches more than honour; none shirked the issue in the poor man's dreams of wealth. All these they put aside to strike a blow for the city. Counting the quest to avenge her honour as the most glorious of all ventures, and leaving Hope, the uncertain goddess, to send them what she would, they faced the foe as they drew near him in the strength of their own manhood; and when the shock of battle came, they chose rather to suffer the uttermost than to win life by weakness. So their memory has escaped the reproaches of men's lips, but they bore instead on their bodies the marks of men's hands, and in a moment of time, at the climax of their lives, were rapt away from a world filled, for their dying eyes, not with terror but with glory.

(43) Such were the men who lie here and such the city that inspired them. We survivors may pray to be spared their bitter hour, but must disdain to meet the foe with a spirit less triumphant. Let us draw strength, not merely from twice-told arguments—how fair and noble a thing it is to show courage in battle—but from the busy spectacle of our great city's life as we have it before us day by day, falling in love with her as we see her, and remembering that all this greatness she owes to men with the fighter's daring, the wise man's understanding of his duty, and the good man's self-discipline in its performance—to men who, if they failed in any ordeal, disdained to deprive the city of their services, but sacrificed their lives as the best offerings on her behalf. So they gave their bodies to the commonwealth and received, each for his own memory, praise that will never die, and with it the grandest of all sepulchres, not that in which their mortal bones are laid, but a home in the minds of men, where their glory remains fresh to stir to speech or action as the occasion comes by. For the whole earth is the sepulchre of famous men; and their story is not graven only on stone over their native earth, but lives on far away, without visible symbol, woven into the stuff of other men's lives. For you now it remains to rival what they have done and, knowing the secret of happiness to be freedom and the secret of freedom a brave heart, not idly to stand aside

from the enemy's onset. For it is not the poor and luckless, as having no hope of prosperity, who have most cause to reckon death as little loss, but those for whom fortune may yet keep reversal in store and who would feel the change most if trouble befell them. Moreover, weakly to decline the trial is more painful to a man of spirit than death coming sudden and unperceived in the hour of strength and enthusiasm.

(44) Therefore I do not mourn with the parents of the dead who are here with us. I will rather comfort them. For they know that they have been born into a world of manifold chances and that he is to be accounted happy to whom the best lot falls—the best sorrow, such as is yours to-day, or the best death, such as fell to these, for whom life and happiness were cut to the self-same measure. I know it is not easy to give you comfort. I know how often in the joy of others you will have reminders of what was once your own, and how men feel sorrow, not for the loss of what they have never tasted, but when something that has grown dear to them has been snatched away. But you must keep a brave heart in the hope of other children, those who are still of age to bear them. For the new-comers will help you to forget the gap in your own circle, and will help the city to fill up the ranks of its workers and its soldiers. For no man is fitted to give fair and honest advice in council if he has not, like his fellows, a family at stake in the hour of the city's danger. To you who are past the age of vigour I would say: count the long years of happiness so much gain to set off against the brief space that yet remains, and let your burden be lightened by the glory of the dead. For the love of honour alone is not staled by age, and it is by honour, not, as some say, by gold, that the helpless end of life is cheered.

(45) I turn to those amongst you who are children or brothers of the fallen, for whom I foresee a mighty contest with the memory of the dead. Their praise is in all men's mouths, and hardly, even for supremest heroism, you will be adjudged to have achieved, not the same but a little less than they. For the living have the jealousy of rivals to contend with, but the dead are honoured with unchallenged admiration.

If I must also speak a word to those who are now in widowhood on the powers and duties of women, I will cast all my advice into one brief sentence. Great will be your glory if you do not lower the nature that is within you—hers greatest of all whose praise or blame is least bruited on the lips of men.

(46) I have spoken such words as I had to say according as the law prescribes, and the graveside offerings to the dead have been duly made. Henceforward the city will take charge of their children till manhood: such is the crown and benefit she holds out to the dead and to their kin for the trials they have undergone for her. For where the prize is highest, there, too, are the best citizens to contend for it.

And now, when you have finished your lamentation, let each of you depart.

Index

Analysis and interpretation of histories: aims, 27–38; basic questions, 12–13; materials, 13–20; principles of relationship, 20–27
Anglo-Saxon Chronicle, 13–14, 17–18
Aristotle: and Dewey, 139, 142–43; dramatic analysis, 56; *Rhetoric*, 152–53, 164–65

Barth, John, *The Floating Opera*, 94 n.
Beard, Charles and Mary, *The Rise of American Civilization*, 25–26
Berkeley, George, *Siris*, 34
Booth, Wayne C., *The Rhetoric of Fiction*, 154 n.

Carlyle, Thomas, *The French Revolution*, 32–33
Causation in histories, 21–27
Circular definition, 130–31 n.
Conflicts in drama, 68 n.
Conrad, Joseph, *Lord Jim*, 94–95
Context of interpretive reading, broadening of, 171–72

Descartes, René, *Meditations*, 99, 154 n.
Descriptive history, 15, 17
Dewey, John, 139–50; and Aristotle, 139, 142, 143; and Hume and Plato, comparison with, 140–43; *Logic, the Theory of Inquiry*, 144, 155; relationship, as principle in, 140

Dewey's *Human Nature and Conduct*, analysis and interpretation of Sec. I of Part One, 144–50; arts, 146; causation, physical and moral, 148; civilization, 149; consequences, future, 148, 149, 150; continuity, 146; future and past, as poles of a process, 148; individual and society, 147; intelligence, 147, 148, 149; interaction, 146; personal and subjective factors, 150; physiological functions, 144–45; process, 146–49; sharing, 147; situation, 147; social environment, 147
Drama: questions of analysis, 54; questions of interpretation, 53–54; special problems in reading, 88–91
Drama and fiction, historical writings and, 51–53
Dramatic manner, 91–93

Events, historical, 13, 17, 18
Exhaustive distinction, 106 n.
Explanations in histories, 21–27

Facts, historical, 13–20; events, 13, 17, 18; qualities, 13, 18–20
Fiction, special problems in reading, 91–98
Funeral Oration of Pericles. *See* Pericles' Funeral Oration, analysis and interpretation of

191